PROBLEMS IN POLICING

JOHN ROBERT CENCICH, J.S.D.

THE HAGUE PRESS INTERNATIONAL

Library of Congress Cataloging-in-Publication Data
Cencich, John R., 1957 –
   Problems in Policing /John R. Cencich (ed.)
   Pages cm (studies in crime and public policy)
   ISBN 978-0-9913293-0-4   (paperback)
   1. Federal Bureau of Investigation *Law Enforcement
   Bulletin.*
   2. Community oriented policing. 3. Problem solving
   policing.
   3. Hot spots. 5. Crime. I. Title.

Printed in the United States
The Hague Press International
First Edition

Contents

INTRODUCTION

By

John Robert Cencich, J.S.D.

SOLVING PROBLEMS IS THE NAME OF THE GAME FOR POLICE OFFICERS. There is no other profession in our nation that combines intense training in law, community relations, and defensive tactics with broad duties that include the authority to make life and death decisions in a literal heartbeat.

Modern policing began when the London Metropolitan Police Force was officially formed in 1829 after a bill was introduced into Parliament by Sir Robert Peel. Before that, the Bow Street Runners served writs of attachment and capias ordered by magistrates. Founded by Henry Fielding in 1749, these plainclothes "constables" arrested criminals ranging from petty thieves to cold-blooded murderers. The bodies of the accused were produced before the Bow Street Magistrates Court, which operated out of Number 4 Bow Street near Covent Garden. After having been found guilty, many convicted felons were sent to the American colonies up until 1776 when the Revolutionary War brought those "correctional" activities to a halt.[1]

The deeds and acts of the Bow Street Runners are well known, and sometimes infamous. Men like Thomas

Carpmeal and Moses Morant[2] investigated serious crimes on the gritty streets of London. I was fortunate to have been given a private tour of both the Bow Street Magistrates Court and Scotland Yard's famous Crime Museum (previously known as the "Black Museum")15 years before the court—with its Metropolitan Police detail—closed its doors for official business in 2005.

I served a special attachment with the Met in the early 1990s, and I can say without question that these men and women are second to none. I have recently learned from my colleagues in London that the Bow Street premises are now scheduled to be converted to a new police museum, which will also house the nearly century and a half old Crime Museum.

The Bow Street Runners were ultimately amalgamated with the Met, which as previously noted, was founded by Sir Robert Peel. Peel, who became known as the father of modern policing, had a vision for police reform. While the police were to be organized along military lines, the officers themselves were ordinary civilians with special responsibilities. And the citizens themselves were considered integral parts of the policing function. Indeed, Peel called on the police to inform the public of crime news in a timely fashion. He also called for the officers to be hired on a probationary basis, to be properly trained, well-groomed, and above all, to have command of their temper.

In the end, "Peelian Reform" viewed police success through the absence (or minimization) of crime rather than the number of "collars" made by the officer on the beat. To better reflect its community-oriented policing mission, the Met eventually went from being known as the Metropolitan Police Force to the Metropolitan Police Service.

It is without question that the creation of a modern force for the policing of the London metropolis had a major impact on American policing. While there were night watchman and wardens working in places like New Amsterdam, it was not until 1833 that an independent police force was established in the United States.

Modeled to some degree after the London Metropolitan Police, the city of Philadelphia created a 24-hour police force in 1833. Five years later, the city of Boston followed suit, as well as New York City in 1845. In fact, in our nation's capital the primary police force, which was established in 1861 under President Abraham Lincoln, is still known as the Metropolitan Police of the District of Columbia.

The presence of certain customs and terminology of the Met can still be seen in the United States. The term cop or "copper" came from the copper buttons on the police constable's uniform. Interestingly, when I was a police officer in Virginia, the magistrates (who we addressed as "squire"), typed the initials "P.C" after our names on arrest warrants; thus, identifying us by the old title of "police constable."

Today, all civilian police officers in the United States are "commissioned." A commissioned officer is one who has broad authority. Their authority, while certainly subject to later review, is such that decisions may be taken on the spot without further authorization. In some countries the level of authority increases in rank, and in many cases full authority is not realized until an officer is "commissioned" into the senior officer ranks.

Another difference between policing in the United States and that of our colleagues in many parts of the world, is that general policing is left to the individual American states and territories. In other words, we have no national police force. This is a matter of constitutional law. Consequently, each state—through its legislative body—decides exactly how policing responsibilities will be distributed. Generally speaking, the most local police agency has primarily responsibility within its jurisdiction.

This means that the Pittsburgh Bureau of Police, for example, has primary jurisdiction in the city of Pittsburgh, even though the Allegheny County Police and the Pennsylvania State Police both have jurisdiction (as do others) in the city. In general terms, federal officers and agents have the authority to enforce federal laws only.

Most federal law enforcement agencies share the same authority to enforce federal laws. For example, special agents of the drug enforcement administration (DEA) and the Bureau of Alcohol, Tobacco, Firearms and Explosives (ATF) have the exact same authority to arrest persons suspected of committing federal crimes and to execute federal search warrants. The principal difference is the statutory authority to investigate specific federal crimes.

It is without question that the Federal Bureau of Investigation (FBI) has broad investigative responsibility. But in addition to purely federal crimes, the military criminal investigative organizations (MCIOs)—such as the Naval Criminal Investigative Service (NCIS) and the Air Force Office of Special Investigations (OSI)—have primary responsibility for investigating crimes that are not normally associated with federal jurisdiction. These offenses include child abuse, sexual assault, homicide, armed robbery, and arson involving persons subject to the Uniform Code of Military Justice, and their authority and jurisdiction is worldwide.

But whether we are talking about eighteenth century London or modern policing in America's cities, towns, and counties, the focus remains one of problem solving. It is the police officer on the beat, whether on foot, motor vehicle, or horseback, that remains the "backbone" of the police service. Unlike detectives and special agents, these officers aim to apprehend criminals, preserve the peace, and render aid to victims by solving problems, some of which are undertaken on the spot.

This book is about examining contemporary issues of "problems in policing." But it is much more. It is also about taking a "scientific" approach to solutions for those problems. In a 2011 article published jointly by the Harvard Kennedy School's (HKS) Program in Criminal Justice and the National Institute of Justice (NIJ), it was said that a "radical reformation of the role of science in policing will be necessary if policing is to become an arena of evidence-based policies."[3]

I could not agree more. When I first became a police officer in the late 1970s, I was aware of the fact that John Jay College in New York City offered a bachelor's degree in "police science." Leading figures in the field of police science, which later became known as "criminal justice," included August Vollmer and O.W. Wilson. In time, police corruption went down, communications and equipment improved, and police officers began to attend college.

In fact, I took college courses and received police training based in part upon funding from the federal government's Law Enforcement Assistance Administration, which was known at the time as the "LEAA." Many of the functions of the LEAA were eventually taken on by agencies such as the Office of Justice Programs (OJP), the Bureau of Justice Statistics (BJS), and the National Institute of Justice (NIJ).

But substantial assistance in methods of problem-solving for police came in the 1960s from a somewhat unlikely source. Herman Goldstein was neither a police officer nor a professor, although he would indeed become a very accomplished scholar and professor in time. He was an assistant to O.W. Wilson who was then the Chicago Police Superintendent. With research funding from the Ford Foundation, Wilson dissected, analyzed, and synthesized many aspects of policing including the police subculture.

His work resulted in what might been seen as a revolutionary change in policing, which is known as "problem-solving policing." In my view, "community-oriented policing, which you have undoubtedly heard of, is problem-solving policing, yet, problem-solving policing is not always community based. In any event, neither of these concepts is simply about getting out of the patrol car and talking with citizens. Such an activity bears almost no relationship to community policing. It is about solving problems that affect quality of life and crime control. While such an approach involves a lot of common sense, it is nevertheless a complex undertaking. It requires changing organizational cultures, implementing interpersonal skills, and taking a more than average degree of risk.

For these and other reasons, Goldstein's research and methods are as applicable today as they were in the late twentieth century. We now have DNA, fiber optics, advanced information technology, and a new generation of violent and often sophisticated criminals. In the end, the police have problems to solve, and they cannot rely on decades-old research such as the Kansas City Preventive Patrol Experiment by saying that the presence of marked patrol cars has no effect on crime control. Indeed, directed patrols, hot spots, and selective enforcement have all been found to be successful in one way or another in our communities.

I have always had an interest in solving problems as a police officer. That's what proactive officers do. And I believe risk-taking is absolutely necessary. But such an approach must be research-driven and evidence based. Officers must be fully trained and knowledgeable, even-tempered, and armed with compassion and common sense. And that empathy must extend to everyone including victims who have different social beliefs, and often to suspects as well.

What I have done in this book is taken a number of selected articles that address current problems in policing. These articles come from both the FBI *Law Enforcement Bulletin* and publications of the National Institute of Justice. They are followed with critical thinking exercises and discussion questions that I developed. To the extent possible, I have interjected my own experiences in the exercises and questions. I will present dilemmas that I have personally been faced with. Sometimes I sorted the issues out, and there were times that I did not. But that is called experience, and there is nothing like personally understanding the struggles that police officers face on a daily basis and gaining wisdom in the process.

But my experiences are not gratuitous "war stories." I weave my participation and observations into the teaching points. The first objective is to combine reality on the street with critical thinking and scholarship. This approach is followed by a secondary objective, which is to see how you might respond to some of these situations.

Accordingly, we will examine your problem-solving thinking process as an individual, and more importantly, as part of a team. I have every confidence that if you put 100 percent into the course and these problems, you will exceed my accomplishments and successes in police work exponentially, and the valuable experiences you eventually gain from things not working out as planned will be minimal.

ENDNOTES

---

[1] Beattie, J. M. (2012). *The first English detectives: The Bow Street Runners and the policing of London, 1750 -1840.* Oxford University Press.

[2] Id.

[3] Weisburd, D. & Neyroud, P. (2011). Police science: Toward a new paradigm. *New Perspectives in Policing.* Harvard Kennedy School – The Program in Criminal Justice Policy and Management and the National Institute of Justice.
http://www.hks.harvard.edu/var/ezp_site/storage/fckedito r/file/pdfs/centers-programs/programs/criminal-justice/NPIP-Police%20Science-TowardaNewParadigm.pdf

PERSPECTIVE
THE DISEASE OF CERTAINTY
By Everett Doolittle, D.P.A.

March 2012: *FBI Law Enforcement Bulletin*

I HAVE HAD GREAT OPPORTUNITIES OVER MY MANY YEARS in law enforcement. I have served as a police officer, a deputy sheriff, and even the chief deputy, but I found my greatest career opportunity at the Minnesota Bureau of Criminal Apprehension (BCA). At BCA, I tackled my most challenging assignment when I led the Cold Case Unit (CCU).

Early in my career, I gained valuable experience by working on homicide teams. But, studying the errors of others and reworking an old case granted me even greater insight into why cases fail. This article describes one of the major sources of these investigative errors: a phenomenon I dubbed the "Disease of Certainty."

The Disease of Certainty is fatal to investigations. Both inexperienced and seasoned officers can catch this contagious disease, and it can spread throughout a team. It occurs when officers feel so convinced of their own beliefs that they allow themselves to become tunnel-visioned about one conclusion and ignore clues that might point them in another direction. Those who resist the disease may be ridiculed and ostracized for their supposed lack of understanding and inability to see the truth if all of their coworkers share the same beliefs and assumptions about the investigation.

The numerous cases that CCU worked over the years taught us many lessons about the Disease of Certainty. For clarification, when I refer to the BCA CCU, I include all members of the BCA team (agents, analysts, forensic scientists, and support personnel) and the local and county investigators who assist these investigations. Cold case investigations demand a multiagency approach to solve a difficult problem, so a diverse set of personnel with varying expertise comprise the team.

By describing what I have learned about the Disease of Certainty, I do not aim to demean the work of the initial agencies involved, but to help others avoid the same mistakes in the future. I want to eliminate this deadly disease of perception that can prevent investigators from seeing beyond their own assumptions. All of these cases involved dedicated and professional individuals, but fatal errors occurred nonetheless. CCU does not aim to judge the initial investigators but to work with the agency as a team to reinvigorate the investigation. One person or agency never deserves all of the credit for cracking a case because it demands a true team effort.

A CASE STUDY

My work with CCU began with numerous rape and assault cases, but I will focus on a series of homicides. The first of the confirmed homicides occurred in December 1978. As the Huling family slept in their secluded rural farm house north of the Twin Cities (St. Paul and Minneapolis) in Minnesota, an intruder entered their home. Before leaving, the intruder viciously murdered Alice Huling and three of her children—miraculously, one survived.

Several other seemingly unrelated crimes occurred over the following year. The next one took place in May 1979 when Marlys Wohlenhaus came home from school. A few hours later, her mother returned from errands and found Marlys severely beaten and unconscious. The girl was pronounced dead 2 days later. Next, in the following months, a young woman disappeared after leaving a restaurant. Though her car quickly was discovered near the Mississippi River, her body was not found for another 5 years. Yet again, soon after, a young girl left another restaurant where witnesses saw her forced into a vehicle, and her body was found days later.

These cases shocked the surrounding communities. However, because no apparent relationship existed between the crimes, the police departments investigated them individually. Several independent investigations continued for many years. In each of the cases, police identified a different prime suspect who became the central focus of the investigation.

THE DISEASE DEFINED

To understand the seriousness of this issue, I need to explain the investigative process and how problems can arise. There are two logical approaches to problem solving that investigators must understand and use effectively: deductive and inductive reasoning. Deductive reasoning results from the evidence that people see in murder-mystery movies—the smoking gun, witnesses, DNA, fingerprints, and other tangible facts and clues. With deductive reasoning, this evidence builds the foundation of the case, and everything comes together to point to one conclusion.

Unfortunately, most real-life investigations differ greatly from the ones seen on television. In many cases, investigators can gather little if any tangible facts or evidence, which leads to a difficult, complex investigation that quickly can become a cold case. In these instances, investigators must turn to inductive reasoning to evaluate possible directions and outcomes.

Through inductive reasoning, or scenario-based logic, we determine possibilities and probabilities based on experience and intuition and then attempt to prove or disprove them. Investigators start with a simple question, for example: Who killed Marlys Wohlenhaus? Could it be her boyfriend? What would be his motive? Could it be her stepfather or the neighbor kid who lives down the block? What would be their motives? Investigators attempt to identify possibilities and eliminate them one by one until only the most probable solution remains. To the seasoned investigator, this type of reasoning becomes the routine course of action.

These types of reasoning can go awry when in the mind of an investigator a possibility becomes the only reality. When officers become convinced of a certain solution, they may think that others who disagree with their answer simply do not understand. In most cases, experienced investigators' instincts are correct, and their prime suspect indeed committed the crime. Nevertheless, one always must keep an open mind to the facts that disagree with an initial assessment as probability does not equate to certainty. Anyone can come to an incorrect first conclusion, especially when little or no straightforward evidence exists, and a conclusion is based mainly on conjecture.

THE CASE RESOLVED

In the serial murders outlined above, this Disease of Certainty led law enforcement personnel to disregard key information because it did not agree with their previous conclusions. However, when CCU reopened the case, many new hypotheses developed, and answers were found among the volumes of information the initial investigators had gathered. As in many cold cases, this only could happen when some initial investigators were removed and new personnel were assigned to support the case.

Eventually, CCU solved these crimes by examining a suspect who quickly had been cleared in the initial investigation. This man was not an acquaintance, stepfather, priest, or deputy, but a stranger. Joseph Ture was a drifter who lived in his car at a rest stop about 4 miles from the Huling home. Four days after the murders, police arrested Ture for an unrelated crime and found a ski mask, a club wrapped in leather, and a small toy car in his possession. These items became significant years later.

Two years later, in 1981, Ture was arrested and convicted of the murder of another waitress. While awaiting trial, he supposedly talked to his cellmate about his involvement in the murders of the Huling family and Marlys Wohlenhaus, and his statements were forwarded to law enforcement agencies. When officers questioned Ture, he maintained his innocence and claimed he was working at an automobile plant in St. Paul when the homicides occurred. The investigators contacted the plant and confirmed that a Joseph Ture was working on the assembly line at the time of the murder of Marlys Wohlenhaus. As a result, the officers eliminated Ture as a suspect.

When CCU personnel examined this case 20 years later, however, they reconsidered evidence, such as

Ture's statements to his cellmate and the items he possessed at the time of his initial arrest. They double-checked Ture's alibi and realized that it actually was Joseph Ture, Sr., the suspect's father, who worked at the automobile plant at the time of the murder. Upon further inquiry, CCU members discovered other incriminating remarks that the suspect made to his cellmate. Ture divulged information that only someone with direct involvement in the crime would have known. Also, the team found that Billy Huling, the one surviving child of the Huling home, could identify the toy car found with Ture when he was arrested decades earlier; Billy and his brother, Wayne, had played with a similar one prior to the night their family was murdered.

This example illustrates how investigators can become too convinced of their own conclusions. Because Joseph Ture allegedly was working at the time of the Wohlenhaus murder, officers disregarded other significant evidence against him. Once CCU reexamined previously held truths about the case (such as Ture's alibi), they solved the crimes. This case has appeared numerous times on television.

Dangers of Overconfidence
Over the years, I have seen priests, deputy sheriffs, stepfathers, neighborhood kids, boyfriends, parents, spouses, and other innocent suspects become not only the focus of the investigation but the only possible answer in the minds of investigators. Once investigators develop this mind-set, it takes courage for others to stand up and disagree with the one perceived truth.

Also, this Disease of Certainty seriously can damage innocent individuals who mistakenly become the focus of the investigation. In some instances, little or no factual evidence exists against a suspect, yet the police, community, and media all believe the individual committed the crime. Rather than grieving the loss of a friend, acquaintance, or loved one, the suspect must deal with being viewed as a criminal in the eyes of the public.

Investigators face the challenge of pursuing their work confidently and proactively, yet understanding that they can be wrong and that if they are their errors impact many people. In this way, officers hold much power and influence over the lives of others, and their ethics matter a great deal. Police may want to solve cases quickly by relying on their instincts and investigating aggressively, but they also have a duty to remain open-minded, fair, and thorough. Working cold cases, I have seen the conflicts that arise when these priorities fall out of balance.

CCU's success in identifying Ture as the murderer in no way detracts from the competency of the original investigators. But, to combat the Disease of Certainty, agencies must remember that personnel assigned to a particular case do not "own" that investigation. In the serial murders described above, the initial investigative teams included experienced officers who had long records of success, yet their experience may have contributed to their failures. These errors, while understandable, may not have occurred had the investigators not formed such strong beliefs of who committed the crimes. Experienced investigators draw on their past successes, which may blind them to unexpected possibilities.

A WIDE PERSPECTIVE

Many of the cases worked by CCU, like the Wohlenhaus and Huling murders, involved talented and dedicated personnel who focused too narrowly on one hypothetical conclusion. One incorrect hypothesis should not jeopardize an entire case. Every investigation reveals several paths that can lead in any number of directions, and, if it dead-ends, investigators need to turn around and try a new one. Problems arise, however, when police venture down the wrong path and refuse to see that they are going in the wrong direction.

Once investigators develop this fixed mind-set, they filter out information that disagrees with their conclusion and only see the evidence that supports their answers. I have observed this phenomenon often while managing multiagency task forces and referred to it as the "Don Quixote Effect." Don Quixote, a famous literary hero, mistakenly battled windmills because he believed so strongly that they were giants. This idea resonates in Thomas Kuhn's 1962 book, The Structure of Scientific Revolutions, which discusses the difficulties experienced by scientists when they discovered information that disagreed with their long-held truths or paradigms.

Overconfidence is not the only way that the Disease of Certainty can infiltrate an investigation. Sometimes, a lack of perspective leads the team awry. When investigators dig deeply into the facts of a case, they can become too focused on one suspect, one lead, or one piece of information and lose sight of the bigger picture. This line of thinking caused investigators to mistakenly eliminate Joseph Ture as a suspect in the crimes described above.

When venturing into a densely wooded forest—it is easy to lose sight of the forest when surrounded by trees. Similarly, when officers become bogged down by puzzling information and unanswered questions, they may find it difficult to see the bigger picture of the case. Solving a difficult and complex investigation with keen inductive reasoning demands more than a team of dedicated personnel; it requires a leader. True leaders can see beyond disparate facts and seemingly unrelated evidence to view the whole "forest," and they have the courage to tell others when they are heading in the wrong direction.

CONCLUSION

Because the Cold Case Unit receives cases after a significant amount of time has passed and all initial leads have been exhausted, it brings a fresh perspective to the puzzle. CCU's investigators are not the same team of officers who responded to the scene of the crime, interviewed witnesses, interacted with a grieving family, and felt the pressure of media attention that surrounds high-profile cases; because of this, they may provide a new approach missing from the initial investigation.

Additionally, because CCU receives cases that stumped a dedicated team of investigators, cold case officers know they must consider "out-of-the-box" solutions and, thus, are less susceptible to the Disease of Certainty. A unit, such as ours at BCA, can provide this service for any agency willing to challenge experienced investigators' long-held beliefs and dig into old cases. Agencies must remember that even their most talented officers can fall victim to overconfidence, and this Disease of Certainty may have caused errors in cold cases that still can be resolved.

DISCUSSION QUESTIONS

1. Hungarian Scientist Albert Szent-Gyorgyi said, "Discovery consists of seeing what everyone has seen and thinking what nobody has thought." How do you think such a statement fits with the "Disease of Certainty"?

CRITICAL THINKING EXERCISE

The author of this article makes a very good point regarding the scientific investigative process, but there is much more to this than deductive and inductive reasoning. As a group, develop a short outline on the process to include how hypotheses are formed, and how inductive and deductive reasoning can be incorporated into the process. Be sure to provide short definitions of the terms that you use and how they apply to a criminal investigation.

Law Enforcement Professionalism
Training Is the Key

By Anthony J. Pinizzotto, Ph.D.;
Shannon Bohrer, M.B.A.;
and Edward F. Davis, M.A

April 2011: *FBI Law Enforcement Bulletin*

AMERICAN LAW ENFORCEMENT IS PROFESSIONAL, effective, efficient, and, often, regarded as a model to follow worldwide. Some would hold that a significant factor in the history of this professionalism is training, which imparts the knowledge, skills, and attitudes that form its foundation.

The recent deep economic decline in this country negatively affected city, county, and state governments. In response, these entities made drastic budget cuts that impacted most public service organizations in all - jurisdictions. Law enforcement executives now must reduce budgets that, in many cases, they viewed as inadequate to begin with. Deciding what to cut while, at the same time, continuing to provide adequate safety to their communities and members of their agencies is a daunting task. Historically, chiefs and sheriffs have attempted to cover budget cuts by not replacing members who retire or leave their agencies. Today, this measure may not make up the budget shortfall. Some view decreasing recruit training as preferable to eliminating current employees. Additionally, in-service training frequently is reduced to the minimum state Police Officer Standards and Training (POST) requirements. While often hard to justify, however, training constitutes the glue of effectiveness that forms the foundation for successful law enforcement efforts.

Placing scarce resources up front in training can produce safe, effective, and efficient officers, supervisors, and administrators, which can lessen operating costs in the long run. As an old advertisement for oil filters pointed out, "You can pay me now, or you can pay me later," the idea being that sometimes a small investment can result in large savings. The cost of an oil filter is minor compared with that of an engine. The same holds true for law enforcement training.

NECESSITY OF TRAINING

In many ways, these difficult economic times should cause agencies to reevaluate their training needs, including the topics covered, the methodology used, and the effectiveness achieved. With fewer available resources, law enforcement organizations need to ensure that with their training, they are doing the right thing and doing it the right way.1 What is the cost to a department for an illegal arrest, use of excessive force, or a wrongful death? It seems reasonable to assume that if training could prevent these events, it would be done. Of course, even with the right training, these still can occur. Conversely, without such training these incidents will take place and probably more frequently. Training is rarely viewed from the perspective of risk management, yet a direct relationship exists.

HOUSE OF TRAINING

Thinking of police training as a house can illustrate how to divide the process into four categories. While each has a different purpose, all of the training is interrelated and interdependent, just as the foundation, walls, and roof support and form a structure.

- Entrance-level training (initial knowledge, skills, and attitudes for new officers)

- In-service training (maintenance of skills taught in entrance level, along with knowledge about new laws, enforcement procedures, and safety practices)

- Supervisor training (specific information tailored to overseeing rank-and-file members and to developing instructional abilities)

- Administrator training (influences direction and operational effectiveness of the organization)

The authors offer these four categories of training only as a guide that can represent the training in any agency. Not meant to be all inclusive, these do not encompass every possible training need, but give an overall view. When examining their training needs, agencies should take the overall view because training greatly influences and shapes the interdependency and interrelationships of their officers, units, and

ranks and affects every law enforcement function.

ENTRANCE-LEVEL TRAINING

Viewing police training as a house requires starting with sound raw materials: the recruits. The right training can shape the recruit into a potentially long-term effective and efficient employee. Entrance-level training does not end or finish the training process but, rather, allows the recruit to operate with minimum supervision and to continue learning through experiences and in-service training. Selecting quality recruits is like choosing the best materials to build the foundation of a house. After all, everything else sits on the foundation. Without the proper foundation materials (the recruit and the entrance-level training), the long-term product has no guarantee of success.

MAINTENANCE TRAINING

As with any house, police training must be maintained. This involves the in-service and specialized continuum of training that officers need. Selecting appropriate candidates and providing sound entrance-level training began the process of turning the raw materials (recruits) into the solid structure. When quality recruits receive the correct entrance-level training, they gain the knowledge, skills, and attitudes to become effective and efficient officers for a long time. However, if the training stops at that point, their efficiency can decline. Agencies should view regular in-service and specialized training, just like the initial recruit selection and training, as a long-term investment. Building a house well with a solid foundation creates a positive investment, but, without maintenance, unexpected problems will develop.

SUPERVISOR TRAINING

Even with the proper maintenance, at some point, a house may need remodeling. The same holds true in police training. Oftentimes, agencies select officers who excel at a particular skill to become supervisors and trainers, which does not always work well. Those who mold and build the raw materials (the recruits) into effective and efficient officers and who take seasoned professionals and form them into supervisors and managers need to receive specific training following an extensive selection process. Supervising and instructing others require not only subject-matter expertise but also the ability to accurately convey knowledge to others. Continued training for supervisors and instructors must include evaluating their training skills and how well they apply them.

ADMINISTRATOR TRAINING

The final category, administrator training, frequently is overlooked. Agencies often assume that officers who worked the streets, arrested people, and became supervisors or trainers have gained the necessary experience. Arguments have been made in both directions on this topic, with both having valid points. One argument is that all of the preceding training—as an officer, supervisor, or trainer—helped prepare the individual for the position.

The counter argument holds that all of the previous training was targeted toward those previous assignments, whereas administrative positions require additional skills. Supervisors supervise people and managers manage programs, but administrators need all of these abilities plus leadership. Another valid argument could be made that administrators are the most important because they determine the training content, budget, and direction of their agencies. Administrator training also can prove difficult to obtain because only a few nationally recognized law enforcement training academies, such as the FBI National Academy, offer such courses.

When comparing police training to a house, administrators represent the long-term investment potential that all home owners recognize as the bottom line. Using the best materials, performing continual maintenance, and remodeling portions when needed culminate in a structure that can last through many generations—so also can law enforcement agencies that understand the importance of well-trained leaders who can move their organizations forward through whatever challenges they may face.

CONCLUSION

Training should be viewed as an investment law enforcement agencies make for the present and future. With fiscal restraints, however, it often becomes one of the first casualties. Because training forms the center of law enforcement effectiveness and efficiency, administrators have a fiduciary responsibility to examine the resources they use to ensure that their citizens are getting their money's worth. Questioning their training programs, content, and projected benefits can prove a better course of action than merely halting training altogether. After all, recruiting, hiring, and training officers who work a long and productive career—from recruitment to retirement—represents a lofty goal that every chief and sheriff tries to attain.

By doing so, these leaders can safeguard their communities not only for the short term but for future generations.

ENDNOTES

1 The authors based this article on their personal experiences in the law enforcement profession and on three main references: Peter Senge, *The Fifth Discipline: The Art and Practice of the Learning Organization* (New York, NY: Broadway Business, 1994); Walter Dick and Lou Carey, The Systematic Design of Instruction (Glenview, IL: Scott, Foresman/Little Brown Higher Education, 1990); and Robert Gagne and Karen Medsker, *The Conditions of Learning: Training Applications* (Fort Worth, TX: Harcourt Brace and Company, 1996).

DISCUSSION QUESTIONS

1. This is a very well-written and succinct article. But does it tell us anything new about the necessity of police training?

2. What is the relationship between the notion of civil liability and police training?

CRITICAL THINKING EXERCISE

When I was a patrol officer I participated in what was seen as a revolutionary training program that was called "Roll-Call Training." Later as a detective and subsequently as a special agent, I provided roll-call training to different precincts and police platoons. As a group, research the concept of roll-call training, and be prepared to discuss it in class.

POLICE PRACTICE
BUILDING AN EFFECTIVE PROPERTY ROOM

By Ceaser Moore

August 2011: *FBI Law Enforcement Bulletin*

LAW ENFORCEMENT AGENCIES AROUND THE COUNTRY dedicate themselves to fighting crime, and their leaders seek innovative approaches to investigate and arrest offenders. Too often, however, officers pay little or no attention to what happens to evidence after they arrest a criminal. Every law enforcement officer knows that evidence must be protected and maintained for laboratory examination and presentation at trial, and many assume that their department always does so flawlessly. Yet, the storage facilities that have the crucial responsibility to maintain evidence and property seem to garner attention only after mishaps. To prevent these errors, law enforcement leaders must maintain a well-equipped property room for their agencies.

In early 2007, we at the Houston, Texas, Police Department (HPD) determined that we needed to completely overhaul our old property storage room, built in 1906. In June 2009, after years of planning, designing, and building, we unveiled a state-of-the-art police property and evidence storage facility.

THE HOUSTON EXPERIENCE

CONSTRUCTION PROCESS

First and foremost, we decided on the location, scale, and parameters of our future property room. To ensure an easy transition and to minimize costs, we chose to build the facility adjacent to the old one on a 2.4-acre site in downtown Houston. We then selected an architecture firm that could carry out all of our plans for a reasonable cost. With our chosen firm, we designed a 59,000-square-foot facility with 11,117 square feet of office space and 31,535 square feet of internal storage.

After we finalized these basic logistics, we determined how this new property room would drastically improve the old model. We planned a moveable 16-foot, high-density compact mobile system for evidence storage, 15,277 square feet of exterior covered storage, and 1,141 square feet of freezers that reach 0°F.

Then, we worked with our officers to determine what technology we needed to properly equip the new facility. Based on this research, we installed high-tech security cameras, movable shelving, an inventory control bar coding system, and concrete vaults.

The room also features a self-contained fire system called Early Suppression, Fast Response, which protects high-pile storage commodities in all of the storage areas, and the building is 100 percent covered by sprinklers inside and out. Another suppression system prevents the pipes from freezing in the outdoor and freezer storage areas but delivers water in case of a fire. The facility's other security features include an emergency electric generator, which can handle the power load for the entire building. These additional features ensure that the HPD Property Room functions both securely and efficiently.

After this nearly 3-year design and construction process, in mid 2009, we spent 6 months transferring evidence from our former property room and opened the new facility for operation. We were excited to provide our officers with a property room they can trust to protect the evidence that they work so hard to gather.

In total, the construction of the new facility cost $13.2 million. After this initial investment, the HPD reaps enormous benefits from such a well-equipped evidence maintenance system. In an average year, the property room handles approximately 95,000 pieces of evidence, including money, weapons, electronics, biological evidence, and any other miscellaneous items that have been seized, stolen, or recovered. A staff of 42 employees, both officers and civilians, manages the facility, which operates 12 hours a day, 7 days a week for the public and 24 hours a day for law enforcement.

LESSONS LEARNED

During the move, we identified our highest priority storage items-specifically, money, guns, DNA/biological evidence, files, and flammables/combustibles. Money and guns demand tight security, as these often are targeted in property room robberies. Additionally, DNA/biological evidence requires careful maintenance for laboratory analysis. Advances in DNA technology have clinched court cases and vindicated innocent defendants, but these sensitive items lose their value if not stored properly. Also, many property rooms overlook the importance of proper storage of flammable and combustible materials; fire accelerants must be removed or properly controlled to protect all stakeholders and evidence.

Initially, we did not transfer narcotics out of the old storage facility into the new one. Narcotics qualify as a hazardous item, and the Houston Fire Department maintains specific requirements for facilities that handle large amounts of hazardous material. After ensuring that we followed all necessary protocol to store these items, we transferred all narcotics evidence out of the of property room.

ENVIRONMENTAL FRIENDLINESS

Our department prides itself on strong community relations, so we kept the public's well-being in mind as we designed the new HPD property room. Therefore, we sought to minimize the facility's disturbance on the surrounding environment. We assessed the room's potential environmental impact, which every agency should examine before they build. To guide our efforts, we sought U.S. Green Building Council's Leadership in Energy and Environmental Design (LEED) certification for our building.

The LEED certification ensures that we continue to minimize our environmental impact throughout the design, construction, and operation phases of the facility. As per LEED requirements, the HPD Property Room boasts several environmentally friendly attributes.

- Our contractors used recycled and regional materials throughout the construction process and diverted 75 percent of their construction waste away from local landfills.
- The building's construction supplies included materials extracted and produced locally or within 500 miles of the site.
- A thermoplastic roof reflects 65 percent of sunlight to reduce the mechanical and energy loads. Also, we designed the roof to withstand wind loads in excess of 110 mph.

- Motion-activated interior lighting sensors significantly reduce electricity consumption in less trafficked areas.
- Interior finish materials enhance the indoor air quality.
- The project's location on an urban infill site provides employees with easy access to public transit.

These minor changes add up to major results. Our assessments estimate that the building's energy consumption savings exceed 25 percent versus a conventionally designed building.

Conclusion

Above all, at the Houston Police Department we strive for a culture of continuous improvement in our new property room. We want the facility's personnel to become the best in their chosen endeavor and for our field officers to feel secure that all evidence will be properly handled and maintained.

If your agency holds some interest in building a new property facility in the near future, consider the aforementioned ideas in your plans. Addressing these key areas will focus your efforts on areas that have substantial benefits for your organization.

Discussion Questions

1. How do you see the Houston Police Department's new evidence and property room beyond issues related to the integrity of the evidence?

CRITICAL THINKING EXERCISE

When I was a special agent, I had my own evidence
locker in my office. Often I made drug and illegal
liquor purchases in the middle of the night (or
supervised other buys as a case/control agent). In such
instances, I packaged, sealed, and appropriately
marked the evidence. Since I had a take-home
government vehicle, I typically secured the evidence in
the trunk until the next working day when I secured it
in my evidence locker. I did, of course, notate on the
chain-of-custody record where it had been stored in
the vehicle and the date and time the evidence was
transferred to the evidence locker.

Discuss as a group whether this is a good practice and
how it might be improved. Bear in mind that unlike
the Houston Police Department, not all agencies have
a 24/7 property/evidence section.

Misconduct Allegations: Procedural vs. Distributional Justice

By Mark Carignan, M.P.A.

May 2013: *FBI Law Enforcement Bulletin*

ON OCCASION LAW ENFORCEMENT AGENCIES EXPERIENCE allegations of police misconduct. Administrators must deal with these contentions in a manner that satisfies many different interests. These often conflict, further complicating police commanders' duties.

Senior police leaders must develop complaint processing systems and policies that allow for effective employee management. Detection and investigation of alleged misconduct must consider public approval while not violating labor laws and collective bargaining agreements.

Citizen satisfaction—fulfilling their needs or wants—means many things. This simple description does not define what members of the public expect when they make complaints of police misconduct.

A study of complaints filed against one city's police officers showed that the complaining citizens wanted a variety of results. Of those grievances, 20 percent sought serious consequences, such as the termination or lengthy suspension of the officer. The remaining 80 percent expected retraining or light punishment. Twenty percent of that subset wanted to report the incident and have their complaint heard regardless of the outcome.[1]

"Satisfaction" is a subjective term with different meanings for citizens in varied circumstances. The way agencies handle complaints affects public approval more than the results.

JUSTICE

For decades, social science has explored and accepted the concept of *procedural justice*. This asserts that the process through which an event occurs plays a significant role in the participants' perceptions of fairness regarding the result.[2] How something happens is as important as what takes place. The event could be the establishment of procedure, negotiation of a financial agreement, or settling of a dispute.

Studies have shown that procedural justice regarding dispute handling crosses several aspects of everyday life, such as interpersonal relationships, commercial interactions, citizen-government contacts, and traditional community-police encounters. Procedural justice applies to resolution of complaints of police misconduct. This concept aids in designing policies and procedures that result in higher levels of citizen satisfaction.

INTERACTIONS

Consumers have specific expectations that sometimes go unmet. Service providers often settle grievances with monetary or product-based solutions. This outcome-focused resolution is an example of *distributional justice*. Some commercial interactions do not work with this type of result-oriented justice. In these circumstances, the influence of procedural justice becomes apparent.

In a 2008 study, researchers found that individuals who participated in forming policies had lower levels of dissatisfaction with negative decisions than those who were not involved.[3] Research indicated a reduction in unrealistic expectations when individuals knew that other persons participated in the process. For example, sports enthusiasts who were aware that other fans participated in developing a seat assignment policy had fewer impractical perceptions that certain spectators would get the best seats, whether or not they participated in the process.[4]

In addition to providing an example of procedural justice, this study indicated that reducing dissatisfaction in conflict resolution is as important as increasing satisfaction. This may pertain to encounters with police officers involving citizen complaints of misconduct.

With conflict resolution, the American criminal justice system focuses on distributional justice. People break laws, officers arrest suspects, and the court systems dispense justice. Studies have indicated that satisfaction among participants in this system is distinct. According to the research, procedural justice plays a significant role.

A 3-month study of crime victims found that police officer treatment of citizens was more relevant to their gratification than solving their cases.[5] It included five points to measure satisfaction: 1) overall approval; 2) courtesy and politeness; 3) speed of response; 4) level of concern; and 5) helpfulness. The research indicated that officer courtesy, concern, and kindness directly and positively influenced fulfillment levels, even though they had nothing to do with the outcome. These reflect procedural justice.

Treatment of these citizens—procedural justice—compares with the successful resolution of the crime—distributional justice. In 2002 the average clearance rate, an outcome-based measure of satisfaction, for property crimes in the United States was 17 percent.[6] This indicated a low success rate; however, the study found that 81 percent of respondents rated their overall approval to be 8 on a 10-point ordinal scale.[7] This showed that the treatment of complainants influenced their satisfaction more than the complaint results.

Researchers interviewed 184 citizens to obtain opinions regarding interactions with police officers. Responses fell into one of two categories; the first was a person calling the police to resolve a dispute, and the other involved an officer detaining an individual for a minor motor vehicle violation. The study entailed the outcome of the encounters and the fairness with which the police officer treated the individual.

The results indicated that members of the public cared more about their treatment by police than the outcome of the situation. According to this study, respondents who perceived fair handling gave more positive evaluations than those who alleged unjust treatment, whether the officer solved the problem or cited the person.[8] This study has broader implications because individuals who experienced self-perceived fairness had a positive opinion of police services overall, not just in the particular interaction.

There was a strong correlation between perceived fairness and overall satisfaction during traffic enforcement, regardless of ticketing. Citizens who indicated fair treatment by officers and received tickets reported higher levels of satisfaction than those who felt poorly regarded but only got warnings.[9]

INTERNAL AFFAIRS

Until the 1960s agencies often dismissed allegations of police officer misconduct by reassigning officers or threatening complainants with retribution.[10] Today commanders recognize the need to investigate to maintain the integrity of their agencies and ensure public trust.

The oldest, most common, structured complaint processing system is internal affairs.[11] Conducted by law enforcement employees, inquiries are similar to traditional investigations with witnesses' interviews, document and evidence reviews, and subject examination. The investigating officer prepares a report and forwards it up the chain of command with each higher-level supervisor commenting and making recommendations.

Upon receiving reports and proposals, command-level decision makers accept or refer them back down the chain of command for further investigation or review. Once accepted, management usually assigns one of six dispositions to it.

First, a sustained complaint is one in which the allegations are found to be true. The second disposition is an unfounded complaint where substantial credible evidence exists indicating that the alleged misconduct did not take place. In the third, exoneration, the officer acted as alleged; however, law, procedure, and circumstances authorized the actions.

In the fourth, the complaint receives a classification of not sustained if there is insufficient evidence to support or refute the allegation. Two conclusions that occur less frequently are ending an investigation for exceptional reasons, such as an officer resigning prior to its completion or authorities determining that a police officer is responsible for conduct that is not part of the original complaint.

Internal affairs reports investigation results after establishing a final determination. Complainants get a letter, while subject officers receive official notification and possible counseling, training, or discipline as required.

Similar to a criminal investigation, an internal inquiry is a process through which a third party determines facts and makes a decision. Dispute resolution systems that follow an inquisitional model create low satisfaction levels for those involved.[12] Participants surrender process control—the handling of the dispute—and decision control—the outcome. This loss of power results in a decline in satisfaction for the complainant.

CIVILIAN REVIEW BOARD

A civilian review board (CRB) is a group staffed by civilians that investigates officer misconduct allegations. Their roles vary and may include complaint intake, investigation, advising, or decision making.

At one time CRBs were the best solution for citizen dissatisfaction with the internal affairs system. Advocates thought CRBs increased public satisfaction, perceived legitimacy of investigations, and the number of sustained complaints. They asserted that exposing the internal process to public scrutiny improved investigation quality and complaint support. This supposedly resulted in discipline and training that lowered levels of misconduct.[13] Research and experience indicate that this is not the case.

The rate of sustained complaints under CRBs is statistically lower than that of a traditional internal affairs function.[14] They usually reach the same conclusions as internal affairs' investigations. Discipline recommendations from CRBs prove more lenient than those imposed by department leaders.[15]

CRBs are unsuccessful in increasing public satisfaction. They improve the perception of transparency, but weaken the control of officer misconduct or enhanced complainant gratification.

CRBs aim to unveil the secrecy of internal investigations, not to increase complainants' fulfillment. The purpose of these systems is to improve transparency and public faith in the process. Raising citizen satisfaction is a secondary goal that does not focus on the method of accomplishment.

MEDIATION

Used in divorce settlements, lawsuits, and labor disagreements, mediation has become popular in the United States. It focuses on a face-to-face meeting between disputants, facilitated by a professional intermediary, with the goal of sharing information and views. The purpose is to increase mutual understanding and reach a voluntary agreement.[16] It concentrates on process, with little regard for outcome while the basis is procedural, not distributional fairness.

A 1996 study of alleged police misconduct in Australia found that 35 percent of complainants were satisfied when using mediation. Researchers indicated that 16 percent felt that way with complaints handled in a more traditional manner.[17]

A similar study in the United Kingdom found comparable results with 30 percent of individuals indicating satisfaction with their mediation experience.

None of the people with fully investigated complaints rated their experience that way.[18]

Mediation is not always an appropriate means to process allegations of police misconduct. This method is unacceptable for use-of-force complaints. An analysis of these matters is important, but goes beyond the scope of this article.

POLICIES

Procedural justice principles apply to a wide range of circumstances. The author examined studies, took the broad implications of procedural justice, and pointed them toward citizen allegations of police misconduct.

People are satisfied with systems they consider fair. They believe it is just if they are involved in its design or execution. Studies indicated that this occurs even when they do not achieve the desired outcome.

Police administrators should develop complaint-processing systems that increase complainants' self-perceived involvement while preserving the agency's ability to manage, investigate, and discipline its employees. The most efficient way to achieve this is to construct a hybrid system that embraces the strengths of existing ones while avoiding their weaknesses.

It is important for departments to include complainants in the process prior to the filing of complaints. Involving the public through consultation with community administrators, neighborhood groups, and religious leaders is essential during the design phase. Considering their experiences and opinions is important. However, police administrators must maintain control and make final design and procedural decisions.

It is necessary to provide complainants with a detailed description of the process through which their complaint will travel. With input from the accuser, law enforcement agencies classify grievances to determine the appropriate path. Final decisions regarding the classifications of complaints (e.g., minor, major, criminal) must remain with the commander.

CONCLUSION

There are numerous processes for handling complaints. Mediation is appropriate for a misunderstanding of an officer's actions or intent. Serious allegations, such as an abuse of force, require a formal investigation. It is important that the agency inform the complainant of the system used, the reason chosen, and the process required.

Departments provide complainants with a detailed description of the results informing them of the outcome, investigative procedures, and factors that led to the conclusion. Law enforcement agencies must accomplish this while protecting their employees' rights to confidentiality regarding their employment status, discipline, and training.

Any policy implementation or change requires an ongoing evaluation of its impact. To accomplish this task, after they process the allegations, organizations survey complainants focusing on their satisfaction and faith in the agency's complaint processing ability. It is important to consider police officer concerns when conducting policy studies and evaluations.

It is a requirement for law enforcement agencies to provide citizens with an opportunity to express their dissatisfaction with a police officer's conduct. Departments must strive for the public's satisfaction while maintaining control of employees, protecting their rights, and accomplishing law enforcement functions. A policy for processing citizen complaints must meet all of these needs.

ENDNOTES

[1] M. Sviridoff and J. McElroy, *Processing Complaints Against Police in New York City: The Complainant's Perspective* (New York, NY: Vera Institute, 1989).

[2] E.A. Lind and T.R. Tyler, *The Social Psychology of Procedural Justice* (New York, NY: Plenum Press, 1988).

[3] T.C. Greenwell, E. Brownlee, J.S. Jordan, and N. Popp, "Service Fairness in Spectator Sport: The Importance of Voice and Choice on Customer Satisfaction," *Sport Marketing Quarterly* 17, no.2 (2008): 71-78.

[4] Greenwell, Brownlee, Jordan, and Popp.

[5] R. Tewksbury and A. West, "Crime Victims' Satisfaction with Police Services: An Assessment in One Urban Community," *The Justice Professional* 14, no. 4 (2001): 271-285.

[6] Federal Bureau of Investigation, *Uniform Crime Reports: Crime in the United States 2002,* Table 26 (Washington, D.C.: U.S. Government Printing Office, 2002).

[7] Tewksbury and West.

[8] T.R. Tyler and R. Folger, "Distributional and Procedural Aspects of Satisfaction with Citizen-Police Encounters," *Basic and Applied Social Psychology* 1, no. 4 (1980): 281-292.

[9] Tyler and Folger.

[10] D.W. Perez and W.K. Muir, "Administrative Review of Alleged Police Brutality," in *Police Violence: Understanding and Controlling Police Abuse of Force,* ed. W.A. Geller and H. Toch (New Haven, CT: Yale University Press, 1996).

[11] S. Walker, C. Archbold, and L. Herbst, *Mediating Citizen Complaints Against*

Police Officers: A Guide for Police and Community Leaders (Washington, D.C.: U.S. Government Printing Office, 2002).

[12] W.A. Kerstetter, "Toward Justice for All: Procedural Justice and the Review of Citizen Complaints," in *Police Violence: Understanding and Controlling Police Abuse of Force*. Ed. W.A. Geller and H. Toch (New Haven, CT: Yale University Press, 1996).

[13] J. DeAngelis and A. Kupchik, "Citizen Oversight, Procedural Justice, and Officer Perceptions of the Complaint Investigation Process," *Policing: An International Journal of Police Strategies and Management* 30, no. 4 (2007): 651-671.

[14] E. Luna, "Accountability to the Community on the Use of Deadly Force," *Policing by Consent* 10, no. 1 (1994): 4-6.

[15] Perez and Muir.

[16] Walker, Archbold, and Herbst (2002).

[17] R. Holland, "Informal Resolution: Dealing with Complaints against Police in a Manner Satisfactory to the Officer and the Complainant," *International Journal of Comparative and Applied Criminal Justice* 20 (1996): 83-93.

[18] C. Corbett, "Complaints Against the Police: The New Procedure of Informal Resolution," *Policy and Society* 2, no. 1 (1991): 47-60.

DISCUSSION QUESTIONS

1. From a citizen complaint perspective, what is the distinction between procedural and distributional justice?

2. Due to pressure from rank-and-file police officers, some departments provide a warning to complainants that should their complaint be determined to have been intentionally or maliciously false, they may be subject to criminal prosecution for making a false report to the police as well as open to being sued by the individual officer. Do you think this is a proper practice? Why or why not?

CRITICAL THINKING EXERCISE

During my law-enforcement career I served a 1-year assignment as Special Agent in Charge of the "Office of Professional Standards," which is an internal affairs unit. While we certainly received and investigated citizen complaints, by policy we basically did not provide the complainant with the results of the investigation. This was due primarily to privacy laws and personnel rules and regulations. Consequently, complainants sometimes became upset, and were of the view the matter was "swept under the rug."

Drawing from this article, what are some practices that might be implemented with the view of minimizing the contentiousness with the public over not knowing the results of the internal affairs investigation?

PREDICTIVE POLICING
USING TECHNOLOGY TO REDUCE CRIME

By Zach Friend, M.P.P.

April 2013: *FBI Law Enforcement Bulletin*

NATIONWIDE LAW ENFORCEMENT AGENCIES FACE THE problem of doing more with less. Departments slash budgets and implement furloughs, while management struggles to meet the public safety needs of the community. The Santa Cruz, California, Police Department handles the same issues with increasing property crimes and service calls and diminishing staff. Unable to hire more officers, the department searched for a nontraditional solution.

In late 2010 researchers published a paper that the department believed might hold the answer. They proposed that it was possible to predict certain crimes, much like scientists forecast earthquake aftershocks. An "aftercrime" often follows an initial crime. The time and location of previous criminal activity helps to determine future offenses. These researchers developed an algorithm (mathematical procedure) that calculates future crime locations.[1]

EQUALIZING RESOURCES

The Santa Cruz Police Department has 94 sworn officers and serves a population of 60,000. A university, amusement park, and beach push the seasonal population to 150,000. Department personnel contacted a Santa Clara University professor to apply the algorithm, hoping that leveraging technology would improve their efforts. The police chief indicated that the department could not hire more officers. He felt that the program could allocate dwindling resources more efficiently.

Santa Cruz police envisioned deploying officers by shift to the most targeted locations in the city. The predictive policing model helped to alert officers to targeted locations in real time, a significant improvement over traditional tactics.

MAKING IT WORK

The algorithm is a culmination of anthropological and criminological behavior research. It uses complex mathematics to estimate crime and predict future hot spots. Researchers based these studies on information that officers inherently know. For example, when people are victims, the chance that they or their neighbors will be victimized again increases. Offenders criminalize familiar areas. There are detectable patterns associated with the times and locations of their crimes.

Using an earthquake aftershock algorithm, the system employs verified crime data to predict future offenses in 500-square-foot locations. The program uses historical information combined with current data to determine patterns. The system needs between 1,200 and 2,000 data points, including burglaries, batteries, assaults, or other crimes, for the most accuracy. Santa Cruz, averaging between 400 and 600 burglaries per year, used 5 years of data.

Throughout the experiment the Santa Cruz Police Department focused on burglaries—vehicular, residential, and commercial—and motor vehicle thefts.[2] the system works on gang violence, batteries, aggravated assaults, drug crimes, and bike thefts. It functions on all property crimes and violent crimes that have enough data points and are not crimes of passion, such as domestic violence. Homicides generally do not provide enough data points to produce accurate predictions.

USING THE DATA

To add an extra layer of security, employees transfer the data on designated crime types from the records management system (RMS) to the secure Web-based system. The algorithm requires the date, time, type, and location of a crime. This is public data, which adds another level of security in case someone intercepts the information. No one submits, collects, or uses personal data. The system processes the information through the algorithm and combines it with historical crime data to make predictions.

Staff members log in, just like they do on an e-mail account, and the system generates hot spot maps. For Santa Cruz police, there are 15 hot spot maps per shift. Distributed through roll calls, these maps indicate 500-square-foot locations. Officers pass through these areas when they are not obligated to address other calls. No one dispatches or requires them to patrol the sites; they do it as part of their routine extra checks. Some agencies using the program designate predictive policing units to run patrols, while others use unmarked cars to traverse hotspots.

The Santa Cruz Police Department decided not to mandate the patrols. Personnel thought it would eliminate the feeling of an administrative directive and empower officers to be as proactive as their call levels allowed. When police enter and clear the hot spot locations, they notify dispatch with a designated clearing code. This enables dispatch personnel to collect data on the frequency of the officers' presence in the hot spots.

EVALUATING THE PROCESS

During the first 6 months of the program, the department made over 2 dozen arrests within the hot spot locations. However, the true measure of the program's success is not apprehensions, but the reduction of crime. Santa Cruz police officers indicated an initial 11 percent reduction in burglaries and a 4 percent decrease in motor vehicle thefts. As time progresses, the reductions increase. Over a 6-month period, burglaries declined 19 percent.

The system requires 6 months of data to assess whether the method actually is reducing the crime rate. Because the Santa Cruz police did not introduce any additional variables—no additional officers were hired, shift lengths continued, patrol structure remained the same—the department attributed the crime reduction to the model.

The Los Angeles Police Department (LAPD) tested the method under a controlled experiment. The project scientifically proved the model's effectiveness. The city has a larger population and more complex patrol needs than Santa Cruz. Researchers established the experiment in the Foothill Division with a population of 300,000 people. They compared the predictive policing system with LAPD's best practices.

Similar to the Santa Cruz test, the department distributed maps to officers at the beginning of roll call. On some days analysts produced the maps using traditional LAPD hot spot methods. On other days, they used the algorithm. No one told the officers where the maps came from. Graphically they looked the same.

The algorithm provided twice the accuracy that LAPD's current practices produced. While property crime was up .4 percent throughout Los Angeles, Foothill's declined by 12 percent. Foothill benefitted from the largest crime reduction of any division during the experiment.

People found it hard to understand that an algorithm performed similar to a crime analyst. Eventually, even the most skeptical individuals realized that the method worked. The LAPD expanded the program to other divisions serving a total population of over 1.5 million people. Each one that implemented the predictive policing software achieved crime reduction. The department recognized that the predictive policing system is a large improvement over previously used approaches. When looking at a map from 1 week, the assumption is that the next week will be the same. The computer eliminates the bias that people have.

GAINING SUPPORT

As with any new program, questions and concerns arise. People resist change. The Santa Cruz Police Department worked with officers to develop maps and solicit feedback before implementation of the program. The department emphasized that the program does not replace officer intuition but supplements it.

The Santa Cruz Police Department found that veteran officers usually identify 8 or 9 of the 15 hot spot locations. Newer officers discover 1 or 2 of the areas. This validates skilled police officers' intuition, provides additional targeted locations, and imparts tactical information for new officers. The maps reinforce existing knowledge and inform about targeting locations. They standardize information across shifts and experience levels.

The algorithm combines historic and daily crime information, produces real-time predictions of areas to patrol, and normalizes information among shifts. It eliminates the concern about adequate information sharing. Officers obtaining the daily hot spot maps receive any information they missed due to vacation, illness, or regular days off.

The program shares information graphically. It does not replace the value of senior officers teaching younger ones or the need for roll calls to discuss crime trends. It cannot replace police officers' knowledge and skills and does not remove the officer from the equation. It puts law enforcement in the right time and place to prevent crime.

CONCLUSION

Additional departments in the states of California, Washington, South Carolina, Arizona, Tennessee, and Illinois have implemented the program. In November 2011 Time Magazine named predictive policing one of 50 best inventions for 2011.[3] The Santa Cruz police chief acknowledged the recognition, but said the accolades are less important than the crime reduction. According to the chief, "Innovation is the key to modern policing, and we're proud to be leveraging technology in a way that keeps our community safer."[4]

ENDNOTES

[1] Dr. George Mohler, Santa Clara University, California, and Dr. P. Jeffrey Brantingham, University of California at Los Angeles, California, developed the algorithm (mathematical model) for predictive policing.

[2] George Mohler, P. Jeffrey Brantingham, and Zach Friend conducted the research in Santa Cruz, California.

[3] Lev Grossman, Cleo Brock-Abraham, Nick Carbone, Eric Dodds, Jeffrey Kluger, Alice Park, Nate Rawlings,

Claire Suddath, Feifei Sun, Mark Thompson, Bryan Walsh, and Kayla Webley, "The 50 Best Inventions of 2011," *Time Magazine*, November 28, 2011. *www.time.com/time/magazine/article/0,9171,20997 08-13,00.html*(accessed September 27, 2012).
[4] Santa Cruz Police Chief Kevin Vogel.

DISCUSSION QUESTIONS

1. These are certainly statistics that indicate a relationship between the implementation of the predictive-policing model and crime reduction. If you had to select one key factor relative to why the program was successful, what would it be?

2. The New York City Police Department has been under fire for its "stop and frisk" policies. Based upon patterns of crime activity, officers go into these "hot-spots," looking for suspicious activity. Once observed, the officers undertake a stop and frisk based upon the U.S. Supreme Court's decision of *Terry v. Ohio.*[*] The complaints arise due to the "disproportionate" number of Hispanics, African-Americans, and members of other minority groups who have been stopped by the police. Factually, the stops take place in areas where the crimes are occurring. Notably, the victims generally share the same socio-economic, racial, and ethnic characteristics as the suspects. Based upon this article, we know neither the demographics of the zones where crimes were predicted nor the specific law-enforcement activities engaged in by the Santa Cruz and Los Angeles Police Departments. *Hypothetically speaking, if the particular zone is indeed one heavily populated by minority groups, should the police err on the side of being politically correct or be less responsive to the victims, or is there a middle ground that works?*

[*]392 U.S. 1 (1968)

CRITICAL THINKING EXERCISE

During my years as a uniformed police officer and as a plainclothes "anti-crime" officer, I thoroughly enjoyed making frequent stops and frisks ("Terry stops") and warrantless, on-the-spot searches of people and motor vehicles. Making high numbers of arrests for possession of weapons, narcotics, and other contraband, as well as capturing individuals wanted for outstanding warrants and fugitives from justice for murder, armed robbery, and rape, I did receive a number of complaints, which quite naturally mostly came from the individuals I did not arrest because of the lack of probable cause. Unfaltering, I continued "aggressive policing,"* but was able to lower the complaints that were made. From an anecdotal perspective, I can strongly say that there is a propensity for younger, less-experienced officers to receive more complaints than veteran officers on the street.

As a group, assume that you are on an anti-crime task force, and are engaging hot-spot zones or sectors that are inhabited or frequented mostly by members of minority groups. Design a plan that will aggressively ferret out criminal activity, respect the civil rights of all persons including suspects, minimize citizen complaints, and improve the reputation of the police in the community.

*The term "aggressive policing" should not be taken to mean being verbally or physically aggressive towards anyone, but rather it is the notion of being knowledgeable, skilled, and proactive in fighting crime.

Police Practice
Incorporating Hot-Spots Policing into Your Daily Patrol Plan

By

Gary Hoelzer and Jim Gorman

November 2011: *FBI Law Enforcement Bulletin*

IMAGINE SEVERAL MAJORS AND CAPTAINS POOLING THEIR resources to begin a commercial fishing venture. They buy a fleet of boats, hire well-trained casters, and purchase a beautiful 600-acre lake. Then, they strategize how to catch the most fish and make their business profitable. Experienced fishermen know that the fish do not distribute themselves evenly throughout the water, and, thus, the crew does not disperse the boats evenly throughout the lake. They will use technology or, simply, knowledge of the lake to determine where to drop their lines and nets. Dispersing the boats randomly would be ludicrous and would invite financial disaster on the commercial venture.

Ironically, the strategies that fishermen know would fail in the fishing business mirror those employed by some administrators who deploy patrol officers. They expect their officers to catch criminals with only occasional results. If fishermen fished like such officers patrol, they would catch no haul; but, if officers patrolled like fishermen fish, criminals would go to jail, and crime would decrease. You simply fish where the fish live, and you patrol where crimes occur.

BACKGROUND

"You're poaching!" I first heard those words in 1981 during my field training at the St. Louis, Missouri, Police Department from other officers who accused me and my field training officer of initiating car stops, pedestrian checks, and arrests in their jurisdictions. My field training officer and I were guilty as charged, for we routinely ventured several miles away from our assigned location (a mostly residential area) to patrol a major retail and entertainment strip. As we began the midnight watch, the residents in our jurisdiction turned out the lights; but, in the neighborhoods to our north, the action was just getting started. My training officer realized that other areas needed our additional presence. Other officers remained territorial about their assignments, but the supervisors appreciated our additional presence in that lively section of the precinct.

Like my training officer, in the mid- to late-1980s, criminologists noticed that crime and disorder generally occur in clusters, rather than an evenly spread-out manner, throughout geographical jurisdictions. Experts, with the assistance of Minneapolis police and city officials, conducted an influential study on the clusters of crime and disorder. In that city, only 3 percent of the addresses produced 50 percent of the reported crime.[1] When the police department merely transferred officers out of low-crime areas and into those identified as "hot spots," both crime and disorder decreased. These eye-opening results spawned additional federally funded studies.

Spurred by the success in Minneapolis, the National Institute of Justice conducted the Kansas City Gun Experiment and the Indianapolis Directed Patrol Project. These experiments took the Minneapolis approach even further by instructing officers to employ specific strategies as they patrolled the hot spots, or "dots." By targeting specific crimes in the hot spots, violent crime dropped dramatically while community perception of the police and of the safety of their neighborhoods increased.[2]

By the 21st century, it became clear that incident-based officer deployment more effectively reduces crime and disorder than distributing officers in general geographic areas. A National

Academy of Sciences panel concluded: "(S)tudies that focused police resources on crime hot spots provide the strongest collective evidence of police effectiveness that is now available. On the basis of a series of randomized experimental studies, we conclude that the practice described as hot-spots policing is effective in reducing crime and disorder and can achieve these reductions without significant displacement of crime control benefits. Indeed, the research evidence suggests that the diffusion of crime control benefits to areas surrounding treated hot spots is stronger than any displacement outcome."[3]

FROM GEOGRAPHIC BOUNDARIES TO COPS ON THE DOTS

When large departments with sufficient support personnel identify a hot spot, they typically assign special squads of officers to cover them. An agency might call such a squad a community action team (CAT), neighborhood enforcement team (NET), mobile reserve, or tactical operations. As large departments can handle high demand for service, these teams are deployed to a location for a specified period of time and then move to another hot spot. While such teams are effective when they cover a particular area, they seldom remain a permanent fixture in any location; thus, the ultimate responsibility for a hot spot, even in a large agency, falls to the patrol officer assigned to that area.

The vast majority of law enforcement agencies in the United States employ less than 50 officers and do not have the resources to form action teams to address hot spots. They assign officers to geographical locations to conduct field investigations, traffic enforcement, calls for service, and other services expected of uniformed patrol. For a typical agency to address hot spots, it needs to develop deployment plans that minimize geographical boundaries, maximize incident-based deployment, and maintain general patrol services. In other words, put the "cops on the dots."[4]

**Figure 1. Common patrol
areas circled**

**Figure 2. Cool zone vs. hot
spots**

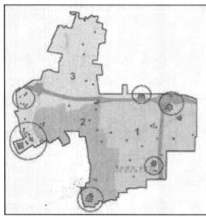 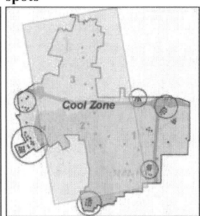

To implement hot-spots policing, agencies first must analyze where crime and disorder clusters in their jurisdictions. Small jurisdictions can chart this effectively with a pin map, but larger agencies need computerized crime mapping. When departments identify a specific problem in a particular geographical area, they highlight it as a "common patrol area," or CPA. To execute CPA deployment, agencies should-

- determine geographical hot spots for crime and disorder;
- designate the sectors responsible for patrol;
- develop strategies at the operational level to address the crime or disorder problem;
- analyze the issue for community input and involvement;
- determine if the CPA will be a permanent designation due to an at-risk location (e.g., retail centers) or temporary due to an ongoing crime spree;
- direct routine patrols to the CPA without requiring permission to cross geographical sector boundaries; and
- track the numbers of patrols and outcomes.

Once a department identifies a CPA, the adjoining sectors share responsibility for the area, which adds supervisor patrols and support units. This system more than triples the number of patrols in CPAs, but maintains reasonably quick response times in low-incidence locations.

OUR EXPERIENCE

Located in the heart of the St. Louis metropolitan area, the Town and Country Police Department (TCPD) transitioned from traditional geography-based to incident-based patrol deployment using CPAs. The department still assigns patrol officers to geographical sectors, but CPAs make an officer's boundaries more fluid. With incident-based deployment, TCPD integrates the intuition and knowledge of experienced patrol officers, like my field training officer, into formal organizational plans.

Early in 2010, TCPD further reduced the emphasis on geographical assignments with the Positioning Units Strategically in Hot Spots (PUSH) program. The program was developed to build on the CPA concept in one particular location, an 11-square-mile city in the St. Louis suburbs. Three sectors (with one officer to patrol each) comprised the jurisdiction, but it was mostly a "cool zone" that experienced little criminal activity.

With PUSH, we consolidated the three sectors into an east patrol and a west patrol and then assigned one officer to each. This leaves the third officer unassigned to any one geographical area so that supervisors can "PUSH" this officer to a location when a problem emerges.

The PUSH plan focuses on clusters of incidents (the dots) as the primary basis for deployment, rather than geographic boundaries. Our latest crime maps illustrate that most dots appear in the southwest or northeast portions of the east patrol; thus, PUSH officers concentrate in those areas.

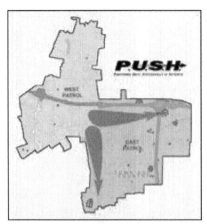

Figure 3. P.U.S.H. deployment plan

The PUSH program functions like a fictitious war room in World War II movies. In these scenes, military personnel huddle around a large table with long poles in their hands, constantly pushing small shapes around on a map to symbolize moving manpower and resources. As commanders receive intelligence from the field, they move assets accordingly. This fluid approach capitalizes on all available manpower to saturate a hot spot.

TACTICS AND STRATEGIES

Targeting the most frequent crimes in a hot spot proves much more effective than merely sending more officers to a problem area.[5] To supplement the increased patrols, supervisors must develop specific strategies for the CPAs based on the area's most frequent crimes. We analyze crime data by location and time of day, and as soon as we observe a pattern, we tailor our approach to that CPA. This system allocates resources more effectively as we equip officers with the appropriate technology and training to address the specific incidents that occur in those areas.

For example, at TCPD, we designate all malls and shopping centers as CPAs due to the increase in organized retail theft; therefore, officers target this crime when they patrol these areas. Officers partner with store security, issue "no trespass" warnings to identified thieves, install license-plate-recognition technology, conduct foot patrols, and target repeat offenders; they also have developed a business watch network.

These tactics specifically target organized retail theft and, thus, reduce crime in malls and shopping centers.

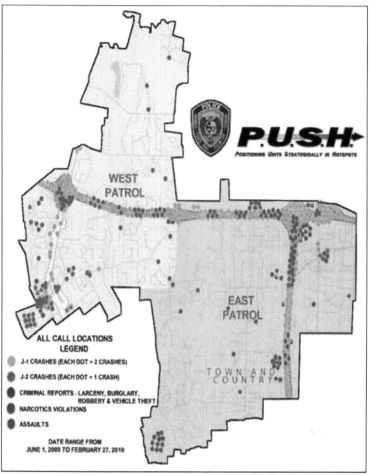

Figure 4. Crime and traffic crash activity

Similarly, in 2009, our department noticed increasing reports of "car hopping," or walk-by thefts of items from parked vehicles. We tailored our patrol in those areas where our crime analysis revealed that car hopping occurred frequently. In one such area, an arterial roadway running through the center of Town and Country, residents reported thefts from vehicles, garages, and homes in the overnight hours. Shortly after we identified the common patrol area, a sergeant patrolling along the roadway around 3:00 a.m. observed a vehicle that resembled one of those sighted in previous thefts. The officer stopped the car in a residential area and identified three occupants who had, in fact, been arrested approximately 1 year earlier for other burglaries and thefts from vehicles. After he apprehended the driver for driving with a suspended license, the officer communicated the intelligence to our detectives. They, in turn, investigated the suspects' involvement in the related crimes.

Even further, CPA and crime-targeted patrols grant officers the opportunity to use their own ideas, expertise, and experience to develop strategies for different areas. The approaches that officers can apply to a CPA are as extensive as their imaginations, including all of the tools that community policing and problem solving bring to the "war-room table."

DATA-DRIVEN APPROACHES TO CRIME AND TRAFFIC SAFETY

Incident-based deployment relates not only to criminal activity but also to important public safety issues, such as traffic crashes. When we include traffic incidents on the crime map of Town and Country, the number of dots explodes [see Figure 4]. Six miles of interstate highway run through the city, and this hot spot of crash activity costs millions of dollars and several hundred injuries annually. When we discovered these results, we realized the need for a unit for interstate traffic enforcement and crash reduction. Simply by including crash data in our incident-based deployment analysis, we identified a dangerous public safety issue and took steps to remedy the problem.

The National Highway Traffic Safety Administration studies these issues all around the country through the Data-Driven Approaches to Crime and Traffic Safety (DDACTS) program. Because crimes often involve motor vehicles, and highly visible traffic enforcement deters crime, the program integrates location-based crime and traffic crash data. DDACTS then studies this data and employs geomapping to identify areas with high rates of crime and crashes. This approach closely mirrors incident-based deployment, and it provides an effective strategy to both fight crime and reduce traffic accidents and violations.[6]

CONCLUSION

These economic times challenge law enforcement agencies to accomplish more with fewer resources. To respond to this conundrum, at the Town and Country Police Department, we embrace the philosophy of incident-based deployment, or hot-spots policing. We reduced the number of officers unoccupied during their patrol by deemphasizing geographical assignments or consolidating them and using the extra officers to patrol hot spots, allowing us to maximize limited resources and control crime. These deployment plans also wed policy with practice by capitalizing on the latest academic research on situational crime prevention. Hot-spots policing, like our PUSH program, efficiently allocates an agency's resources to those that need them most, whether the agency employs 5 officers or 5,000.

ENDNOTES

[1] David Weisburd and Anthony Braga, eds., *Police Innovation: Contrasting Perspectives* (Cambridge: University Press, 2006).
[2] Dennis P. Rogan, James W. Shaw, and Lawrence W. Sherman, "The Kansas City Gun Experiment, *"National Institute of Justice: Research in Brief* (Washington, DC, January 1995).
[3] Wesley Skogan and Kathleen Frydl, ed., *Fairness and Effectiveness in Policing: The Evidence* (Washington, DC: National Academies Press, 2004), 250.
[4] Jack Maple and Chris Mitchell, *The Crime Fighter: How You Can Make Your Community Crime Free* (New York, NY: Doubleday, 1999).
[5] Steven Chermak, Edmund McGarrell, and Alexander Weiss, U.S. Department of Justice, Office of Justice Programs, National Institute of Justice, *Reducing Gun Violence: Evaluation of the Indianapolis Police Department's Directed Patrol Project*, NCJ 188740
(Washington, DC, 2002).
[6] U.S. Department of Transportation, National Highway Traffic Safety Administration, and U.S. Department of Justice, Bureau of Justice Assistance, National Institute of Justice, "Data-Driven Approaches to Crime and Traffic Safety (DDACTS),"*http://www.nhtsa.gov/DOT/NHTSA/Traffic%20Injury %20Control/Articles/Associated%20Files/811186.pdf*(accessed September 12, 2011)

DISCUSSION QUESTIONS

1. Do you think the citizens of a city such as Pittsburgh would support the concept of hot spots policing?

2. Assuming that this proactive policing technique was successful in the reduction of crime, why might there still be objections? What could the police do to minimize objections and maintain the successful program?

CRITICAL THINKING EXERCISE

Discuss as a team how you would deploy officers in a city of the size and population of Pittsburgh with a similar number of zones (elsewhere called precincts or districts). The second part of this exercise is to discuss how such deployments would be managed.

CROWD MANAGEMENT
ADOPTING A NEW PARADIGM
By Mike Masterson

August 2012: *FBI Law Enforcement Bulletin*

MANAGING CROWDS IS ONE OF THE MOST IMPORTANT tasks police perform. Whether or not members of the public agree with this practice, they often judge how well law enforcement officers achieve this—if it is done fairly and effectively. Of course, officers should treat everyone with respect and courtesy without regard to race, gender, national origin, political beliefs, religious practice, sexual orientation, or economic status. Although perhaps daunting, the primary function of police is relational, whether they respond to a domestic dispute, investigate a crime, enforce a traffic regulation, or handle a crowd. Once officers understand this, they will find it easier to determine what to do and how to do it.[1]

LESSONS LEARNED
Studied by law enforcement for at least 40 years, crowd control is important due to the dangers posed by unruly gatherings. To this end, it proves fair to ask whether police leaders do all they can to share lessons learned and incorporate best practices into crowd management philosophy, training, and tactics.

As a young police officer in Madison, Wisconsin, in the 1970s, the author experienced the Vietnam War's aftermath at home and the eruptions of student unrest.

A state capital and home to a major university, Madison at times is a hotbed for protests. From antiapartheid demonstrations and dismantling of shantytowns on capitol property to an annual alcohol-laden Halloween festival, the author, along with fellow officers, monitored and managed partiers and protesters for over four decades. With groups ranging from 6 church members to 250,000 people celebrating in a city park, Madison police successfully balanced rights to assembly and free speech with citizen and officer safety.

The author benefited from those lessons on crowd management when becoming chief of the Boise, Idaho, Police Department in 2005. The city subsequently hosted the National Governors' Conference and the 2009 Special Olympics World Winter Games. Boise police officers manage a wide variety of protests, parades, and demonstrations on issues, such as immigration, human rights, and most recently, a death penalty execution and Occupy Boise.

A police chief's involvement and direction prove critical to officers' ability to successfully manage emotional, potentially volatile crowds. The message received from top-level management greatly influences the behavior and mind-set of frontline officers. Shaping these attitudes begins with a solid understanding that police work involves building relationships with members of the public whom officers are sworn to serve and protect.

BRITISH INFLUENCE
The International Association of Chiefs of Police (IACP) and the Police Executive Research Forum (PERF) have an increasing amount of information available on best

practices in crowd management. PERF's recent publication *Managing Major Events: Best Practices from the Field* contains insight offered by law enforcement leaders from the United States and Canada on what has worked for them.[2]

This report includes the Vancouver, British Columbia, Police Department's new policy on tolerance and restraint when dealing with crowds. Police leadership in Vancouver recognized the success of British crowd control policies, sent their senior executives overseas to study the model, and brought back trainers to assist officers with implementing this new style of crowd control during the 2010 Winter Olympics.

With British input, Vancouver police developed a meet-and-greet strategy. Instead of using riot police in menacing outfits, police officers in standard uniforms engaged the crowd. They shook hands, asked people how they were doing, and told them that officers were there to keep them safe. This created a psychological bond with the group that paid dividends. It becomes more difficult for people to fight the police after being friendly with individual officers.[3]

British research on policing crowds confirms the strategic need for proactive relationship building by police. In the 1980s, a professor at the University of St. Andrews in Scotland published early findings on how law enforcement tactics shape crowd identity and behavior.[4]

Later, a doctor at the University of Liverpool published research on hooliganism—rowdy, violent, or destructive behavior—at British soccer games. Named after fans of a soccer club involved in two riots with South Wales Police in 2001 and 2002, the Cardiff Approach is based on two leading theories of crime reduction—the Elaborated Social Identity Model

(ESIM), the leading scientific theory of crowd psychology, and the Procedural Justice Theory (PSJ).

The ESIM maintains that crowd violence escalates if people think police officers treat them unfairly. PSJ proposes that group members comply with the law when they perceive that officers act with justice and legitimacy.[5] When a crowd becomes unruly and individuals perceive unfair treatment by law enforcement officers, violence can escalate, and a riot can erupt. Recent research finds support for both perspectives and concludes that when police officers act with legitimacy, disorder becomes less likely because citizens will trust and support law enforcement efforts and behave appropriately.[6]

THE MADISON METHOD

Modern research supports a philosophy of public order policing from the 1970s referred to as The Madison Method of Handling People in Crowds and Demonstrations.[7] This approach begins with defining the mission and safeguarding the fundamental rights of people to gather and speak out legally. The philosophy should reflect the agency's core values in viewing citizens as customers. This focus is not situational; it cannot be turned on and off depending on the crisis.

Law enforcement agencies facilitate and protect the public's right to free speech and assembly. When officers realize they are at a protest to ensure these rights, they direct their responses accordingly, from planning to implementing the plan. Officers must have a well-defined mission that encourages the peaceful gathering of people and uses planning, open communication, negotiation, and leadership to accomplish this goal.

Los Angeles Police Department (LAPD) commanders achieved success in planning and communicating their agency's mission during an Occupy Los Angeles gathering. Throughout the event, officers' objective was to facilitate the peaceful removal of all people and their belongings from the city hall park area. Participants received a reasonable amount of time to leave, after which officers issued a dispersal order. Anyone refusing to exit the park faced arrest.[8]

Officers should begin with constructive engagement, dialogue, and a soft approach. British law enforcement agencies call this the "softly-softly approach." Law enforcement personnel mingle and relate to the crowd using low-key procedures based on participants' behavior, rather than their reputation or officers' preconceived notions of their intent.

Police and demonstration organizers should coordinate prior to an event. This re-enforces law enforcement's role as facilitator, rather than confronter. Maintaining dialogue throughout the event helps minimize conflict. Of course, dialogue involves two-way conversation— sometimes this means listening to unpopular opinions and suggestions. There is only one crowd; however, individuals comprise that mass. If the event is peaceful, officers should remain approachable to, for instance, give the location of the nearest ATM, provide the phone number for a taxi, or supply directions to a parking lot.

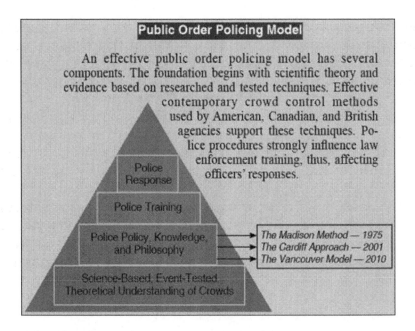

Public Order Policing Model

An effective public order policing model has several components. The foundation begins with scientific theory and evidence based on researched and tested techniques. Effective contemporary crowd control methods used by American, Canadian, and British agencies support these techniques. Police procedures strongly influence law enforcement training, thus, affecting officers' responses.

Police Response

Police Training

Police Policy, Knowledge, and Philosophy

The Madison Method — 1975
The Cardiff Approach — 2001
The Vancouver Model — 2010

Science-Based, Event-Tested Theoretical Understanding of Crowds

Officers must avoid donning their hard gear as a first step. They should remember lessons learned from the 1960s civil rights movement and Vietnam War protests. Police should not rely solely on their equipment and tools.[9] Experience shows that when used as a primary tactical option in public order policing, dialogue is invaluable. Law enforcement officers must defuse confrontations to ensure strong ties with the community. If they fail, rather than stronger community goodwill, the effect will be less civility and the erosion of constitutional rights.[10]

NEGOTIATION AND EDUCATION

Officers must negotiate, educate, and maintain continual dialogue with organizers and crowd members. Police personnel initially must state that they defend the public's right to demonstrate, but cannot allow the crowd to hurt others or destroy property. Whether officers support the crowd's position or if the group holds an unpopular view, law enforcement agencies must remain neutral and prevent physical injuries or property destruction. If arrests become necessary, police officers must respect individuals and avert harm to anyone in custody. Officers must convey that they expect cooperation in return.

Recently, an elected leader in Boise recognized the need for officers to address crowd management questions. It became apparent that some demonstrators misinterpreted law enforcement agencies' approach. While police engaged in reasonable, steady conversation, the public sometimes saw this as uncaring, which indicated the importance of educating demonstrators early. In Vancouver, officers quickly relayed to Winter Olympics fans the strategy to keep everyone safe.

PROTECTION AND PROFESSIONALISM

Protecting officers who work with a crowd is important. The Stockholm, Sweden, Police Department uses highly visible and identifiable "dialogue police," while British law enforcement agencies use "communication police." The Boise Police Department, maintains a tactical unit with full protective equipment on standby in an out-of-sight location near the demonstration. The unit serves as an emergency response to protect officers and the public from harm. Its mission is to safeguard people first and property second. Deploying the emergency response team is a last alternative when soft crowd control tactics prove ineffective.

Law enforcement agencies can show leadership in preparation and training for events by using specially qualified police officers. The best officers to use in crowd control situations are those specifically selected and trained who have the personality to use a soft approach under difficult circumstances. Self-control proves essential.

Not all police officers can manage multitudes

effectively. Crowd control offers a rare opportunity for agencies to cultivate a positive public image. When officers operate as a team, the public observes confidence and professionalism far above any uniformed presence.

ACCOUNTABILITY AND VISIBILITY

While restraining from the employment of force is important, its use may become necessary at large gatherings, especially those born out of passion. Officers working at large events must realize that someone watches and records all arrests. Police officers with up-to-date training in making team arrests ensure efficient apprehensions.

Avoiding the use of outside agencies can be wise. Officers from other locations may differ in philosophy, training, or ability to work together during a conspicuous event. External resources could lack soft crowd management experience or community knowledge. It proves important to local agency leaders that officers take personal responsibility for crowd management in their city.

Occasionally, outside help proves necessary. A recent event in Boise required the participation of five large agencies consisting of state, county, and city forces. The effort was well-planned and coordinated. Success came from all stakeholders' early planning and clear understanding of the mission.

Avoiding anonymity and promoting accountability are essential. By ensuring police officers assigned to crowd control are identifiable, with names and badge numbers clearly visible, agencies prevent their officers from becoming anonymous agents. Obscurity or depersonalization of officers encourages negative crowd behavior and leads to unaccountable actions.

Agencies should videotape events. Segments recorded by participants, bystanders, and media are useful; however, when departments record their own documentation, they ensure its value for case review, accountability, and context. The University of California, Berkeley, Police Department has such a practice. Normally, it videotapes all demonstrations or crowd situations to ensure complete records of the event. During periods in which violations, police actions, or other significant activities occur, the agency employs at least two video cameras.[11] To safeguard the First Amendment and privacy rights of those participating in the event, agencies should adopt a policy governing retention and destruction of these tapes.

During high-profile or large demonstrations, police command officers must remain on the scene, visible, interactive, and willing to take charge. This provides an excellent opportunity to assess the mood of the crowd and reinforce the agency's outlook and crowd management tactics.

COMMUNICATION AND PREPARATION

With 24-hour news, cell phone cameras, Facebook, Twitter, and hundreds of other social media connections, it becomes important to prevent potentially dangerous rumors from appearing as facts. Because of erroneous witness statements and other misleading or false information, justifiable use of force has triggered riots.

Law enforcement agencies play a major role in responsibly reporting accurate information quickly and continually for the benefit of officers, the public, and the media. Although officers are not responsible for inaccurate reporting, developing a proactive, engaged media plan is important. Social media serves as an excellent way to directly communicate department messages and obtain information on events.

Law enforcement agencies must have a plan to de-escalate conflict situations. If an arrest becomes necessary, the individual taken into custody should be one who threatens the peace of the event. Sometimes, officers disperse a crowd to preserve harmony and prevent injuries and property damage. Police officers with specialized skills and equipment do this best. Law enforcement agencies must prepare for circumstances that suddenly can turn a crowd confrontational.

At any large demonstration, law enforcement officers primarily serve as peacekeepers facilitating lawful intentions and expressions. Participants perceive the legitimacy of police actions based on how officers interact with the crowd throughout an event. Communicating expectations, negotiating continually, and emphasizing the goal of safety are vital. Officers should not confuse the actions of a few with those of the group. Law enforcement personnel must remain firm, fair, and professional.

CONCLUSION
Commonplace instant, mass, and social media provide an opportunity to highlight and improve the public's view of law enforcement legitimacy. Using communication and best practices in crowd management, officers reinforce their position as peacekeepers. Police, the most visible form of government, must continue to ensure that the First Amendment rights of the public they serve are protected and guaranteed.

ENDNOTES
[1] D. Couper, *Arrested Development: One Man's Lifelong Mission to Improve Our Nation's Police* (Madison, WI: Dog Ear Publishing, 2012).

2 D. LePard, *Managing Major Events: Best Practices from the Field* (Washington, DC: Police Executive Research Forum, 2011).
3 LePard, *Managing Major Events.*
4 S.D. Reicher, "The St. Paul's Riot: An Explanation of the Limits of Crowd Action in Terms of a Social Identity Model," *European Journal of Social Psychology* 14 (1984): 1-21; and S.D. Reicher, "Crowd Behavior as Social Action," in J.C. Turner, M.A. Hogg, P.J. Oakes, S.D. Reicher, and M.S. Wetherell, *Rediscovering the Social Group: A Self Categorisation Theory* (Oxford, UK: Basil Blackwell, 1987).
5 C. Stott, "Study Identifies Best Approach to Policing Football Matches," *University of Liverpool, UK, University News*, October 20, 2011, *https://news.liv.ac.uk/2011/10/20study-identifies-best-approach-to-policing-football-matches/?utm_source=University+News&utm_medium=email&utm_term=26-10—11&utm_campaign=fortnightly+update* (accessed April 19, 2012).
6 C. Stott, "Crowd Psychology and Public Order Policing: An Overview of Scientific Theory and Evidence" (presented to the HMIC Policing of Public Protest Review Team, University of Liverpool, UK, School of Psychology, September 2009).
7 The Madison Method of handling people in crowds and demonstrations was created by Chief David Couper, Madison, WI, Police Department, and staff in the 1970s.
8 U.S. Department of Homeland Security, Federal Emergency Management Agency, Incident Management System, Incident Command System (ICS) Form 202, National Commander's Intent, Occupy Los Angeles, November 29-30, 2011.
9 L. Reiter, "Occupy and Beyond: Practical Steps for Reasonable Police Crowd Control," Legal and Liability Risk Management Institute (LLRMI), *http://www.llrmi.com/articles/legal_update/*

2011_ crowd_control.shtml(accessed December 13, 2011).

[10] A. Baker, "When the Police Go Military," *New York Times*, December 3, 2011,*http://www.nytimes.com/2011/12/04/sunday-review/have-american-police-become-militarized.html?_r=1&sq =When%20the%20Police%20Go%20Military&st=cse* (acc essed June 19, 2012).

[11] University of California, Berkeley, Police Department, "Crowd Management Policy,"*http://administration.berkeley.edu/prb.PRBCro wdPolicy.pdf* (accessed December 12, 2011).

DISCUSSION QUESTIONS

1. Given the recommendations in this article, do you believe that most modern police departments would take such an approach?

2. Do you think there would be any major differences in the approaches to crowd control between urban or suburban police departments, or rural sheriffs and/or state police forces? Explain your position.

CRITICAL THINKING EXERCISE

This article is based upon the demonstrators' legal right to assemble as guaranteed under the First Amendment of the Constitution. There is no question in my mind that most—if not all—of the recommendations of the author are spot on.

For this exercise, and working as a group, assume that the assembly is indeed unlawful. This could mean the demonstrators did not obtain a proper permit, are trespassing on private property, or another factor other than a lawful demonstration that happened to turn unlawful due to acts of violence or disorderly conduct.

Based upon concepts discussed in this article, develop a plan for handling the initial contact with an unlawful group, but where there is no violence or threats of violence at that moment.

Revitalizing
A Business District From the Inside Out
Green Bay Police Department, Wisconsin
Fort Howard District

U.S. Department of Justice
Office of Justice Programs
National Institute of Justice
(2000)

Themes **The Problem: An inner city business district had** become a high-crime area marked by litter, broken liquor bottles, and people living on the street who were often drunk and disorderly.

Analysis: Officers discovered a high concentration of crime compared to the rest of the city and a disproportionate demand for police and rescue services. Analysis of police records indicated that approximately 20 people were involved in most of the neighborhood complaints. Furthermore, neighborhood residents and business leaders had lost faith in the police to respond to disorder in the area.

Response: Police spearheaded a community effort to strongly enforce public ordinances on open intoxicants, evictions from city parks, trespassing in city parks, and lewd and lascivious behavior.

They also worked to increase liquor license regulation,

mobilize citizens to attend city council meetings, modify the environmental design, use the court system to link alcoholics with treatment resources, and gain the cooperation of liquor store and tavern owners in denying alcohol to habitually intoxicated people.

ASSESSMENT: After a problem-solving initiative began in 1995, Broadway Street was transformed into a booming business district. From 1993, when there were no community police officers in place, to 1999, after police officers had been in place for 4 years, the area experienced a 65-percent reduction in total police calls and a 91-percent decrease in the demand for rescue squad services to handle injuries resulting from assaults. From 1995 to February 2000, the Broadway business district gained more than $8.4 million in new public and private investment, 410 new jobs, and 33 new businesses.

SCANNING

In the city of Green Bay, Wisconsin, Broadway Street had a seedy reputation. People lived on the street, were often drunk and disorderly, and slept on park benches outside of neglected, decaying buildings. Liquor bottles littered the streets. For 4 decades, taverns known for the frequent disorderly behavior of their patrons were not held accountable.

In fact, 16 to 18 taverns—the scene of multiple shootings, stabbings, and other violent crimes operated in Broadway's 3-block business district. Broadway became known as the "Wild West," and law-abiding citizens avoided the area and most area businesses suffered financially.

Residents and business owners in the area viewed Broadway as isolated. They felt abandoned by city government. Before 1995, there was little growth in the Broadway business district.

ANALYZING THE PROBLEM

In 1995, the Green Bay Police Department adopted the concept of community policing. Two officers were assigned to the Fort Howard district, which includes the Broadway business district. Green Bay's community-policing officers (CPO's) focus on long-term problem solving and typically are not dispatched to calls-for-service.

The newly stationed CPO's, Bill Bongle and Steve Scully, met face-to-face with neighbor- hood residents, schoolteachers, children, and business people. Within a short time, the officers learned firsthand about the problems plaguing the Broadway area:

- A disproportionate demand for police and rescue services compared to the rest of the city.
- An unusually high concentration of crimes, including battery, disorderly conduct, retail theft, property damage, public urination, prostitution, and drug activity.
- Visibly intoxicated people in city parks and in close proximity to the nearby elementary school engaging in inappropriate behavior (sleeping on benches, vomiting, urinating, and defecating outdoors).

PEOPLE LIVING ON THE STREETS AND IN THE TAVERNS

An analysis of police offense reports revealed that approximately 20 individuals, mostly habitually intoxicated people who lived on the streets and people who had mental illnesses, were responsible for most of the neighborhood complaints. The homeless shelter had referred many of these individuals to the Brown County Mental Health Center's Alcohol and Other Drug Abuse outpatient counseling. Many of the people living on the street did not use or access these services and remained on the street, though they would have been permitted to stay at the shelter if they had become sober.

Analysis of police data showed that most victims of serious crimes in the area, such as stabbings, shootings, and assaults, were patrons of the problem taverns. Several high-profile incidents, involving violent behavior, drug activity, and prostitution, took place at the Broadway taverns.

In 1993, two men were shot; in 1996, detectives uncovered a child prostitution ring; in 1997, there was a violent attack with pool sticks; in 1998, five people were stabbed in a bar fight; and in 1999, a bar manager was arrested for selling cocaine from a Broadway bar. Repeat calls were made to the same licensed liquor establishments for fights and other alcohol- related problems. Victimization rates were very low for citizens in the area who did not patronize the taverns.

LOOSELY REGULATED LIQUOR LICENSES

Wisconsin State law provides a judicial process for local governments to regulate liquor licenses. Unfortunately, the Green Bay city government rarely exercised its authority to revoke or suspend the licenses of poorly-operated taverns. In fact, the city's Protection and Welfare Committee, which regulates liquor licenses, often approved and renewed licenses in the area without question. In some cases, convicted drug dealers were granted bartender licenses.

The progression of disciplinary action against an owner of a problem tavern amounted to a series of warning letters issued by the Committee. Before 1995, no liquor license had been revoked since the late 1970's. The Committee declined to take action against a problem bar unless the police issued the bar owner a citation.

But under existing city ordinances, police officers could not issue a citation to a bar owner if the owner was absent at the time an incident occurred. As a result, bar management practices and absentee owners contributed to an environment that fostered disorderly and illegal conduct. Under the existing licensing system, it was difficult to hold owners accountable for activities that occurred in their bar.

POLICE ENFORCEMENT LACKING

The police response to alcohol-related complaints in the Broadway business district rarely included arrests, partly due to jail policy. In the early 1990's, the local jail refused to accept prisoners who had blood alcohol content levels higher than .30 percent, unless they had received medical clearances. This eliminated what was known as the "drunk tank" and left no other practical alternative for street patrol officers.

As a consequence of the policy, police spent their time transporting intoxicated people who had been arrested for offenses such as disorderly conduct to a hospital emergency room to receive medical clearance. Police would then transport them to the Brown County Jail or the Brown County Mental Health Center, which provided detoxification. These facilities often released people to the community after 24 hours, where police officers would find them in the same condition soon after their release. Patrol officers viewed the 2 hours spent transporting arrestees from place to place as a waste of time and taxpayer dollars.[1]

During their analysis, the CPO's learned that the neighborhood lacked faith in the police. At meetings sponsored by the Fort Howard-Jefferson Family Neighborhood Resource Center, a bilingual, multicultural, grassroots organization with a commitment to strengthen the Broadway neighborhood, CPO's listened to area business leaders and neighborhood residents. Community members said Broadway was viewed as a dumping ground by the rest of the city, including the police, and its business community had long ago lost faith in the police department's response. Citizens no longer called to report nonemergency problems to the police.

The Green Bay Police Department's analysis showed that the police department had not reached out to other government agencies— such as the revenue department, park department, city attorney's office, building and health inspection departments, and mental health services—that were available to help them address problems in the neighborhood.

Officers also had not been aware of the different roles that municipal and circuit courts could play in resolving disorder problems. Officers in Green Bay can divert offenders to circuit court, but they are encouraged to send minor offenses to municipal court to generate fines. However, the circuit court can order offenders into treatment while the municipal court cannot. The officers met with the Brown County District Attorney, who agreed that people who were habitually intoxicated should be diverted to circuit court, which has broad sentencing authority, including alcohol treatment and probation.

ENVIRONMENTAL DESIGN FLAWS

A review of building design in the Broadway area highlighted numerous deficiencies. Several taverns had dark alcoves and doorways facing alleys, permitting criminals discrete, easy access to the taverns. Drug users and sellers could quickly duck into taverns and get lost in the crowd, making it difficult for patrol officers to make arrests. Poorly designed landscaping created hiding places for people who were intoxicated and living on the street. Dense undergrowth made detection of transients during routine surveillance difficult.

RESPONSE

The Green Bay Police Department developed a response strategy designed to achieve the following goals:

- Eliminate illegal activity from the neighborhood.

- Reduce calls for police and rescue services.

- Bring business to the neighborhood by improving the public's perception of the Broadway business district.

- Restore faith in the police department by building a cooperative working relation- ship with the community.

To achieve these goals, the officers implemented the following five initiatives.

NO-SERVE LIST

The police identified and targeted a core group of individuals who accounted for most of the problems in the area. Officers Bongle and Scully provided liquor store and tavern owners with a list of people who were habitually intoxicated, accompanied by a letter from the police department requesting that licensees deny service to them. The police department placed persons on the list if they met the following criteria:

- Had three or more arrests in a 3-month period in which intoxication was a factor.
- Had been incapacitated by alcohol, requiring detoxification three or more times in a 3-month period.
- Were involved in some type of behavior in the Broadway business district that generated a complaint to the police.

The police department's letter was approved through the city attorney's office. To gain compliance with the no-serve list, police educated liquor retailers and tavern owners on their responsibility to decline service to intoxicated people. The letter defined intoxication by physical characteristics.

The American Civil Liberties Union (ACLU) sent a letter of complaint to the police department, expressing concern over distribution of the no-serve list. The ACLU argued that "Targeting some individuals to be denied legal goods and services causes a tangible change in the legal and social status of the affected individuals."

The ACLU requested that the police department retrieve the lists from bar owners and issue a directive to prohibit the practice in the future. However, the Green Bay City Attorney reviewed the ACLU's complaint and advised the police department that the no-serve list was supported by Wisconsin statute 125.12(2)3, which prohibits distribution of alcohol to "known habitual drunkards." The police department continued the practice, which turned out to be one of the most successful initiatives implemented by the Fort Howard district's CPO's. People who at one time generated three to four calls per day to the police now rarely have police contact.

The officers also targeted specific bars that had a history of a high volume of calls-for-service. In some cases, bars in the area had generated more than 200 calls to the police in a 1-year period, compared with 11 calls from other bars in the area. Bar owners argued, however, that targeting bars with high call volumes would punish bar owners and employees who made legitimate calls for help. To alleviate the concerns of bar and liquor store owners who might become reluctant to call police when there was a disturbance, the police and business owners agreed that calls for assistance would not be used against the businesses.

OPERATION "HOT SEAT"

For this element of their response strategy, Officers Bongle and Scully stepped up enforcement of ordinance violations in the neighborhood. Police issued citations and arrests for activities that would have resulted in warnings in the past. For an offense such as disorderly conduct, the officers used their discretion to send offenders to circuit court, which has the authority to order alcohol treatment.

Several offenders were placed on probation, and Officers Bongle and Scully worked closely with probation officers to enforce probation conditions. These included such restrictions as no alcohol consumption and no visits to taverns or liquor stores. If the officers observed a probationer violating these restrictions, they would report the violation to probation officers, who would have the probationer incarcerated.

MODIFYING ENVIRONMENTAL DESIGN

During analysis, it became clear that no attention had been paid to environmental design in the areas experiencing problems. For this element of the strategy, the police department and other city agencies made the following changes:

- Trimmed overgrown shrubs that concealed illegal activity.
- Modified the Broadway district's park benches to prevent people from lying down.
- Eliminated access to an unsecured apartment building that people who lived on the street used as a hiding place.
- Maintained the Broadway district's park grounds, eliminating buildup of litter and bedding generated by people who lived on the streets.
- Improved lighting in dark alcoves behind taverns and modified rear doors to permit exit only.

OPERATION "SPOTLIGHT"

The police department sought media coverage for its problem-solving efforts. Police believed the media would present a positive story if they were approached early.

The police department explained that arrests, liquor license hearings, and crackdowns were part of the revitalization and improvement of the neighborhood. The department pointed out that many crimes, such as muggings, were rare. A strong relationship was built with the media, who became an asset to the police department by covering the positive change the department was making as well as the trouble businesses and individuals. The press was a useful tool for the department to use against businesses and individuals who did not want to be identified to the public as problems.

INCREASED REGULATION OF LIQUOR LICENSES

Police felt that many citizens were unaware of the licensing regulations governing liquor establishments. Therefore, the community- police response included educating citizens about how they could influence the actions of the Protection and Welfare Committee, which had the power to issue and rescind licenses.

Officers Bongle and Scully provided citizens with dates and times of Protection and Welfare Committee meetings, the names and telephone numbers of council members who sat on the Committee, and the proper procedure for addressing the Committee. Meetings once conducted in a small room in city hall had to be moved to city council chambers in 1996 to accommodate the increased number of citizens attending. The neighborhood's interest in the Committee's actions increased Committee members' accountability to the public.

The police department worked with the city attorney's

office to enforce new city ordinances. Police officers now can cite bar owners even if they are not present when offenses are committed. The city attorney's office developed a system in which points are assessed against the liquor license upon conviction of an alcohol-related offense.

Now, the municipal court can automatically suspend a license and close a tavern for a designated period of time after 12 points have been accumulated.

ASSESSMENT

During the past 4 years, the health of the Broadway business district has steadily improved. Five taverns rife with criminal activity were closed because of the joint efforts of community-policing officers and citizens. By pressuring council members to take action, citizens played a key role in driving out the taverns. Community- policing efforts drove out other troublesome businesses, including one where illicit drugs were sold.

IMPROVED PUBLIC PERCEPTION

Since 1995, the Broadway business district has experienced substantial growth in new businesses and jobs. When 'On Broadway,' a private, nonprofit organization that promotes investment in the Broadway business district, analyzed changes in the neighbor-hood from 1995–99, it discovered the following:

- $8.4 million had been invested by both public and private interests.
- 410 new jobs had been created.
- 33 new businesses had been formed.
- A $1.8 million day care center was under construction.
- $3.1 million had been devoted to streetscape, sidewalk, and lighting improvements by the city government.

REDUCED NEED FOR POLICE AND EMERGENCY SERVICES
Computer-aided dispatch system statistics show a significant decrease in the demand for police resources, including:

- A 65-percent reduction in total police calls from 1993 to 1999.
- A 91-percent decrease in calls for rescue squad services from 1993 to 1999.
- An 86-percent reduction in disorderly conduct calls from 1993 to 1998.
- A 70-percent decrease in disturbance- unwanted person type calls from 1993 to 1998.

This reduction in the demand for police resources frees police officers to assist in other areas of the city.

RESTORED PUBLIC FAITH IN THE POLICE
To educate and mobilize neighborhood residents, the Green Bay Police Department built a close, cooperative working relation- ship with the Fort Howard-Jefferson Family Neighborhood Resource Center, which sponsored neighborhood meetings and handled mass notification of city hearings. This relationship helped the Green Bay Police Department to restore the public's faith in its ability to solve problems in the Broadway district. Cleaning up the area of drunks, taverns, and alleys and bushes played a part in restoring faith, as well.

Dale Smith, owner of Dale's Millennium Motors, a Broadway district business, notes, "Our neighborhood is easily 100 percent better because of the beat cops and their extra efforts." Tom Perry, associate editor of the *Green Bay Press Gazette,* wrote, "Forget the negative images, the news from Broadway is mostly positive and upbeat."

Broadway has become not a part of town that needs to be avoided, but rather "a great place to shop," according to Larry and Ben Frye, owners of the Broadway district's String Instrument Workshop.

DID CRIME RELOCATE?

Although some taverns chose to relocate to other areas of the city, the taverns ceased to pose a problem because they were no longer in the same neighborhood with their problem patrons. However, the habitually intoxicated people did move to areas of the city where enforcement was less stringent. As a consequence, these neighborhoods have asked for and received community-policing teams assigned to their districts.

The Broadway business district now is a thriving part of downtown Green Bay. The Green Bay police had responded to the same calls in the Broadway business district for decades with no change. Only when the police employed a problem-solving approach and sought the assistance of the community did long-lasting changes take place.

FOR MORE INFORMATION

For more information about the Green Bay Police Department's efforts, contact Officers Bill Bongle and Steve Scully at the Fort Howard District, Green Bay Police Department, 307 Adams Street, Green Bay, WI 54301; phone: 920–448–3332; fax: 920–448–3333; e-mail: Bill Bongle: beatcop@msn.com,   Steve Scully: sscully@execpc.com.

NOTES

1.   One individual, who had been placed at the mental health center more than 80 times for intoxication, is estimated to have cost the city some $96,000, as follows: The Brown County Health Center estimates the cost of an admission for detoxification at $400 per day, with an average stay of 2 days; St. Vincent's Hospital estimates hospital emergency room costs to average $300 to $400 for this type of visit; and the police department's business manager estimates the cost of each call to average between $50 and $100,

depending on the number of personnel hours required.

DISCUSSION QUESTIONS

1. The burden of proof for shutting liquor licensed premises down is typically a "preponderance of evidence" rather than proof beyond a reasonable doubt. Do you think the lower standard is good, or perhaps unfair to the bar owner?
2. Due to their pervasively regulated nature, liquor licensed premises are subject to administrative searches without warrants, and evidence of criminal offenses found in the process is admissible in a criminal court. Do you think this is a good practice or should search warrants be required?

CRITICAL THINKING EXERCISE

Every state handles liquor enforcement differently. Some delegate these matters to local police while others utilize state investigators with full police powers to handle issues such as drug distribution, prostitution, and illegal gambling on the premises. Most often state agents, local police, and code enforcement officers team up to work what are known as "nuisance bars." I have worked undercover alone in bars and clubs where I purchased narcotics and illegal liquor, participated in illegal gambling activities, and placed prostitutes and outlaw bikers under surveillance. It is exciting, but also dangerous. I have also worked with multi-jurisdictional teams to shut down nuisance bars. To be successful with either approach, well-coordinated and thought-out plans are necessary. For this exercise, develop two plans. The first is an undercover operation for drug sales in a bar located in a high-crime area. The second involves a team or multijurisdictional enforcement approach that complements the undercover operation. Remember Officer Safety in both plans!

POLICING LIQUOR ESTABLISHMENTS
A HOLISTIC APPROACH
By John L. Gray

November 2010: *FBI Law Enforcement Bulletin*

A SMALL AMERICAN TOWN OF 17,000 RESIDENTS HAD ONE of the highest crime rates in the county. By day, it was a vibrant cluster of small retail shops with residents and visitors enjoying the friendly feeling. At night, however, a different personality emerged: a climate of street fights, open-air drug deals in the parking lots of bars, impaired drivers, property damage from vandalism, and minor thefts had existed for several years.

One bar in a large building had live music and catered to patrons in their early 20s. This establishment had fights that often included the bar's employees nearly every night in the parking lot. Rumors of sexual activities and drug dealing constantly surfaced. In another part of town, local residents patronized three bars in close proximity to each other known as the Bermuda Triangle. When told to leave one establishment, they would walk to another and continue drinking. Police received numerous complaints of drug dealing, fights, and property damage.

Nearly every night, all of the town's police officers, with assistance from state and county personnel, would go from one call to another about alcohol-related crimes, which depleted resources from other areas and increased response times. The town needed a new approach as the police leadership and the city's elected officials continued to hear complaints from the community and crime statistics were not improving.

THE STRATEGY

One proven method of making a community safer involves attacking the locations of crime and disorder. Being proactive early to prevent problems offers the most options for success. To this end, the author presents a strategy for police executives to consider that includes adopting the right mind-set, knowing who is responsible, partnering with other authorities, establishing a point of contact, agreeing upon expectations, training business employees, visiting the establishments, and documenting service calls.

THE RIGHT MIND-SET

The idea that assisting a bar in becoming successful, addressing issues of over service, or preventing disorder in such establishments belongs exclusively to the state's licensing authority on alcoholic beverages constitutes a common misconception. These state agencies often are underfunded and have insufficient personnel to effectively monitor the vast number of licensees. The agents often can handle only the "biggest fire" and, therefore, must react to problems.

When police departments adopt the mind-set, from the executive to the patrol officer, that this is our problem and, therefore, our responsibility, real and lasting results can happen quickly. This mind-set will help form relationships, inspire working partnerships, and create determination to achieve success. Without this foundation, everything that follows will have inconsistent and temporary results.

THE RESPONSIBILITY

First, police leaders should research the state's laws and court findings to determine the responsibilities of the liquor establishment. When police managers know the powers and responsibilities of the business establishment and the state's regulating agency, as well as what tools their own departments have, they will be better equipped to make an effective plan and to engage in a working partnership.

For example, is the business accountable for the behavior of customers outside its building and in its parking lot? Who has the power to immediately suspend the business' operations? Can police officers make an arrest for a minor misdemeanor that did not occur in their presence?

THE PARTNERSHIPS

Liquor control agents are the experts and an essential resource in the management of a bar. Many of the state's licensing agencies have a database that provides information that can assist the police department and may include documentation of administrative violations, owners of record, and arrests of impaired drivers that came from the business. Meeting with representatives will encourage sharing information about a bar's problems and its successes. The licensing agency often has resources for training the employees of bars to prevent overservice and manage problems. The police department should learn about this training and participate in it.

Most liquor establishments will make the required changes necessary to improve business safety and will work with the police to create observable results. For the problem business, the police leader can bring in more partners who have regulatory authority, such as building inspectors, fire marshals, health inspectors, public works officials for street and parking issues, gambling enforcement agents, and state and federal revenue officials.

The police department should enforce codes fairly, firmly, and impartially. It should communicate with the prosecuting attorney about the history of problems and the proactive approaches that did not bring the desired compliance because the prosecutor can seek maximum accountability.

Challenging the renewal of a license, either by suspending or revoking it, is the last regulatory option for government. Similar to terminating an employee, this proves appropriate when all other courses of assistance, training, and progressive steps of accountability have failed. A huge undertaking, it will require the political will and financial commitment of the jurisdiction because ramifications concerning loss of tax revenue or the perception that government is "being heavy handed" against a business can occur.

The success of the police department in this regard is based upon the timely and ongoing sharing of information with the elected officials; they need to be kept continually informed. The process of taking away a problem establishment's license may be long and full of obstacles, but, when successful, substantial lasting benefits to the community include reduced crime and disorder and the availability of public safety resources for other priorities.

THE POINT OF CONTACT

Police leaders should appoint one supervisory-level employee as the point of contact on all issues regarding liquor establishments so the business owners, the licensing agency, and the police administration can give and receive information. Larger jurisdictions may have to divide their communities into areas with several points of contact.

As the police department's watchdog for emerging problems, the point of contact also is the face and voice of the department when dealing with the business and partnering with other government organizations. The value of this approach is the consistency of information, care, and communication from the police that can help keep issues firmly in focus.

THE EXPECTATIONS

Being proactive means that the police department's point of contact meets with the owners and managers of liquor establishments before problems occur. Generally, owners want a successful, profit-making enterprise viewed as an asset to the community and, therefore, usually will cooperate with the police department.

The first step involves delivering a personal invitation to the business for a group meeting of liquor establishment managers. This represents a valuable tool because police leaders and owners can get to know each other. This meeting is about explaining what the police department can and cannot do, what it expects from the establishments on addressing problems, and what it can offer in the way of training and assistance to meet the common goal of a crime-free community and a safe business for patrons and employees.

From this meeting, the police department's point of contact should schedule individual meetings with the owner and the business' management team to help create the relationships, address unique issues, and establish the avenues of communication. The management team members should be informed about the principle that if a crime or disorder is predictable in their business, it also is preventable, and they may be held accountable for failing to take appropriate action. The police point of contact should describe how the department will conduct proactive bar checks, how it will handle problems, and what assistance it can provide.

Having an agenda and distributing the minutes of these meetings will create valuable documentation. A written, formal working agreement between the department and the establishment represents a higher level of documentation that can help hold the business accountable.

THE TRAINING

Employees cannot be held accountable for what they do not know. By helping to train the wait staff and bartenders about dealing with problems and understanding expectations, the police department can increase the impact of the value of the lessons. After all, most workers want to be successful and avoid problems that could lead to criminal liability. This training may pay other benefits as well. For example, when officers respond to the business for a complaint, the employees often will be more comfortable cooperating and may provide more information when they have a relationship with the department.

THE VISITS

Knowing that a police officer likely will stop by can prevent many problems. Defensiveness and skepticism often diminish when these visits are not a surprise. These checks are intended to see whether employees are using the training that they received, to communicate to potential problem patrons that the police are available to take action, and to deepen the communication relationship with the department. A worthy goal is to have every bar visited by a patrol officer at least several times a week.

Officers need to know from the department's command staff the importance of doing this work. Conducting bar checks may cause resistance and noncompliance from officers who never have done such duties or fail to see their value. They should be trained on how to conduct patrol checks of bars, what problems to look for, how to deal with intoxicated persons who are not committing a crime, and what solutions and tools they have at their disposal.

The department should inform liquor establishments that undercover operations also will occur throughout the year at different times. It should consider adopting the practice of making immediate custodial arrests for employees who commit crimes because these have a chilling effect on establishments that allow crime to happen. One effective operation, the underage patron sting, often involves a male and female couple underage by more than 12 months. Of course, the department should craft a comprehensive policy and procedure that meets legal standards and the current professional practice.

THE DOCUMENTATION

A 1-page, check-the-box form for officers to document every call to a liquor establishment creates a climate of fairness. In addition to a normal police report, this form includes information as a cross-reference. What makes this tool especially useful is that it requires the officer to determine whether or not the business could have prevented the event. The completed document is distributed to the department's point of contact who does a follow-up conversation with the establishment's management team.

The immediacy of feedback and accountability between the business and the police can prove valuable. For example, when a liquor license is up for renewal or is being challenged, these documents and the department's case reports become the evidence to present at the administrative hearing. Also, reliable data on liquor establishments within the jurisdiction helps to ascertain if perceptions are accurate. Wise leaders will listen carefully to their employees for the reasons behind their judgments but will use sound data before making a decision to target any location of crime for extra attention.

CONCLUSION

For the town in the opening scenario, change occurred when the police department decided to own the problem. Conversations began with the state liquor control agents and the business owners, and a police lieutenant became the point of contact for all information and conversation with the businesses.

An order, backed up by training, was given to all the patrol teams, and the frequency of routine checks increased. The department started undercover operations, and one resulted in 18 arrests on one night alone. The media accompanied officers and publicized the businesses where arrests occurred.

Within 2 years, two of the Bermuda Triangle bars had changed ownership or management, and their operations improved. The ultimate result of the new approach was that the city's crime rate dropped by 25 percent. The sales tax revenue lost by the closure of several bars was offset by the reduced costs of jail and court costs and rebounded within 12 months.

DISCUSSION QUESTIONS

1. Does the notion or suggestion by local authorities that revoking a liquor license, "will require the political will and financial commitment of the jurisdiction because ramifications concerning loss of tax revenue" raise any red flags or policy perspectives?

2. What implications might arise when local authorities train liquor licensees on state laws and regulations and the time comes for a suspension or revocation of a liquor license by state authorities? Consider, for example, a town tax department issuing an amusement tax stamp to a bar owner for an illegal gambling device (being unaware of the illegality of the device), and state authorities later proceeding to take criminal and/or administrative action for illegal gambling? How might any such dilemmas be minimized or eliminated altogether?

CRITICAL THINKING EXERCISE

As a state law-enforcement officer with full police authority for all criminal laws, I worked extensively in connection with licensed and unlicensed bars and clubs in connection with outlaw motorcycle gangs, money laundering, syndicated gambling, narcotics distribution, lewd and indecent conduct, and sales of liquor to drunkards. As pointed out in the article, investigations were often done on a multi-jurisdictional basis, particularly when working with major police departments with outstanding vice, narcotics, and organized crime units, which provide excellent assistance and support to our administrative and criminal investigations. But most often the precise nature and location of our undercover operations would not be revealed to local police in small towns or rural counties due to security reasons. Local officers would, however, almost always be brought in at raid time or to assist in overt enforcement activities, which is a point in time that information might also be shared with locally elected officials. This is one perspective on how one state jurisdiction operated. Indeed, the author of the article correctly points out the need to check laws in specific jurisdictions in order to ascertain the responsibilities of different interested agencies.

Nevertheless, for this assignment you need to identify any "absolutes" or assumptions stated in the article, which may very well be incorrect. The aim is a constructive critical analysis from operational, policy, statutory, and leadership perspectives.

Synthetic Marijuana
By Roland Macher, Tod W. Burke, Ph.D., and Stephen S. Owen, Ph.D.

May 2012: *FBI Law Enforcement Bulletin*

IN FLORIDA, A 14-YEAR-OLD BOY WAS ADMITTED TO THE emergency room after experiencing seizures and difficulty breathing. He and his brother had smoked herbal incense, referred to by local police as Mr. Nice Guy.[1] In another case, a 17-year-old boy in western Texas was hospitalized in May 2010 after smoking synthetic marijuana before school. After feeling sick on the bus ride to the campus, his symptoms became progressively worse. He was admitted to the hospital, treated, and released within the same day.[2] Statistics indicated that emergency room visits across the country due to the use of synthetic marijuana have risen from 13 in 2009 to approximately 560 in the first half of 2010.[3]

In March 2011, the U.S. Drug Enforcement Administration (DEA) temporarily placed five synthetic chemicals—*JWH-018; JWH-073; JWH-200; CP-47, 497;* and *cannabicyclohexanol*—into Schedule I of the Controlled Substances Act (CSA).[4] These substances produce druglike effects that resemble those resulting from *tetrahydrocannabinol (THC), a cannabanoid* and the primary psychoactive ingredient in marijuana, but have distinct chemical structures.[5] Individuals use them to coat herbal blends and then sell these products under such names as K2, Spice, Mr. Nice Guy, Genie, and others.6 Under the DEA's ruling, punishments for the possession or sale of these chemicals mirror those for marijuana. Law enforcement agencies should gain an understanding of synthetic marijuana, its distribution, potential harmful effects, and concerns for officers.

DEFINITION

In 1995, a Clemson University professor used a synthetic compound to conduct research identifying the effects on the brain from cannabinoids. Following the publication of a paper detailing the experiment, the description of the method and ingredients became popular among persons searching for a marijuana-like high. People began spraying the synthetic chemical compound described in the article on dry herbs and then smoking them as they would regular marijuana.[7]

The main chemical used to produce synthetic marijuana is JWH-018 (the initials are those of the professor conducting the Clemson University experiment), similar to THC.[8] The moniker "imitation marijuana" actually may be a misnomer as no psychopharmacological differences exist between this substance and marijuana. Both chemicals are considered cannabinoids, which attach themselves to the *cannabinoid,* or *CB,* receptors in the brain. However, the synthetic compounds and THC differ in levels of potency.[9]

While significantly different, marijuana and the synthetics share many similarities, including their appearance, method of consumption, euphoriclike high experienced after inhaling or ingesting, negative side effects, and the concerns of law enforcement officials regarding the dangers associated with all such substances. The manufacturing of these products proves fairly simple: Individuals produce the synthetic chemicals separately and then spray them onto dry herbs and plants. Their simplistic creation and low cost ($20 to $50 for 3 grams) make synthetic forms of marijuana attractive to users.[10]

Smoke shops and convenience stores across the nation sell synthetic marijuana labeled as incense. Because local dealers, not laboratories, manufacture the products, health officials have concerns. The risk of contamination—and, therefore, negative side effects—increases.[11] In addition to the United States, Britain, Germany, Poland, France, and Canada also have banned synthetic marijuana.[12]

RESPONSE

The DEA has expressed concern about synthetic marijuana's recreational use and its potential for harm, abuse, and addiction. The agency has controlled five synthetic cannabinoids in Schedule I under the temporary scheduling provision of the CSA, placing them in the same category as LSD, heroin, and marijuana.[13] A Schedule I drug or substance has a high potential for abuse, provides no currently accepted medical use in the United States, and lacks accepted safety standards for use under medical supervision.[14]

In addition, the U.S. Food and Drug Administration does not approve for human consumption synthetic chemicals banned by the DEA. The increasing number of poison control center calls—2,500 through mid-December 2010—and emergency room visits from individuals smoking synthetic marijuana prompted the DEA to act quickly.[15]

Research identifying how consuming these chemicals may affect the body exists but has been limited. For instance, a 2011 study noted a variety of negative physical effects resulting from the use of synthetic marijuana. While most effects dissipated after several hours "with no residual adverse effects in many cases," the study did highlight both short- and long-term impacts of synthetic marijuana as causes for concern.[16]

Both prior and subsequent to the DEA's action, many states moved to ban synthetic marijuana. As of March 2011, 20 states had imposed bans either through legislation or administrative and regulatory processes. Additional legislation remains pending in 37 states. Each state differs in terms of how it approaches synthetic marijuana. For example, among states, some have listed it as a Schedule I drug while others have not, definitions of what constitutes synthetic marijuana differ, and penalties (including classification as a felony or misdemeanor) also vary.[17] In spite of the differences, the theme is clear: States see synthetic marijuana as a significant concern.

POTENTIAL HARMFUL EFFECTS

The DEA's recent restriction provides federal regulations that allow law enforcement officials throughout the country to crack down on the use of synthetic marijuana. One state senator recognizes that the illicit drug market will adapt to the bans on synthetic marijuana, perhaps increasing the street demand for the substance; however, he still believes that laws will successfully minimize "the threat to public safety."[18]

According to the American Association of Poison Control Centers, some users of synthetic marijuana have reported "a fast, racing heartbeat, elevated blood pressure, and nausea."[19] In addition, research found that the chemicals in synthetic marijuana "are three to five times more potent than THC found in marijuana," leading to symptoms, including "loss of consciousness, paranoia, and, occasionally, psychotic episodes." [20]

Research in Germany also discovered that synthetic marijuana use can lead to "withdrawal symptoms and addictive behaviors."[21]

One researcher, a toxicologist and the director of the Missouri Regional Poison Center (MRPC), conducted a study on the effects of synthetic marijuana on humans. He has observed over 30 instances in which teenagers have had negative reactions after using the substances, including harmful effects on the "cardiovascular and central nervous systems."[22] One death has potential links to synthetic marijuana—a teenager in Iowa committed suicide after using a synthetic. The young man's friend said the victim "'freaked out' from the drug."[23]

The MRPC expert further concluded that symptoms resulting from use of the synthetics differ from those of marijuana. In addition to the observable symptoms, such as elevated heart rate and blood pressure and muscle twitching, agitation sometimes accompanies synthetic marijuana use. This differs from marijuana intoxication, commonly marked by "euphoria and a sense of detachment."[24] This has led some medical professionals to suggest that, perhaps, attaching the label "marijuana" to synthetic substances could be misleading because they may more appropriately be viewed as "an altogether different...chemical entity."[25]

CONCERNS AND RECOMMENDATIONS
A man from West Virginia overdosed after trying synthetic marijuana in February 2011. Emergency room officials stated that he experienced extreme agitation and had a heart rate of around 200, well over the normal rate of 60 to 100. Doctors were unsure how to treat him because of the lack of available information and research on the substances. Only after contacting a local poison control center did the doctors learn about synthetic marijuana and properly

treat the victim, who made a full recovery.[26] While the lack of information about synthetic marijuana presents a significant public health concern that emergency department physicians must address, a similar issue arises for law enforcement officials. Officers must receive training and information to raise their awareness of synthetic marijuana.

One of the potential problems with synthetic marijuana is the inability to identify the substances or recognize the immediate effects they may have on an individual. One report suggested that the aroma of synthetic marijuana contains elements of mustard, tarragon, oregano, and pepper, with additional similarity to "stale lavender...like an antique shop."[27] The same report also indicated that smoke from synthetic marijuana "smelled nothing like marijuana smoke."[28] This type of information may aid in the identification of synthetic marijuana. With the recent ban of the chemicals associated with synthetic marijuana, law enforcement officers also should be trained to identify the substances and the dangers associated with them. Medical officials should share information with police officers, particularly school resource officers, in hopes that the spread of knowledge will aid in efforts aimed at prevention and treatment of abuse.

Until society becomes better informed, law enforcement professionals and health officials must recognize the risks posed by synthetic marijuana chemicals to individuals. Drug and field tests should focus on helping to identify the substances because standard marijuana screens may not detect the chemicals.[29] This also will allow medical personnel to better treat individuals under the influence of synthetic marijuana.

Further research likely will aid the DEA in its determination of whether these chemicals need to be placed on the federal list of controlled substances permanently and, if so, how they should be scheduled. Although some light has been shed on the negative effects of synthetic marijuana, and the recent DEA ban has given law enforcement officials basis on which to enforce punishment, the future of these substances remains unclear. However, apparently, concerns about the risks of synthetic marijuana will continue as a topic of discussion among legislators, medical professionals, and law enforcement officers.

CONCLUSION
Synthetic marijuana is not the first type of drug that has raised such concerns, nor will it be the last. For instance, attention recently has focused on the abuse of bath salts, which have effects mimicking those of methamphetamine.[30] Regardless, the increasing popularity and evident health risks associated with synthetic marijuana have raised concerns among legislators, medical personnel, and law enforcement officers across the country. The number of unreported cases of negative effects from consumption of synthetic marijuana remains unknown. The DEA designed its recent ban to address these problems, at least temporarily, giving researchers time to study the effects of synthetic marijuana.

ENDNOTES
[1] Linda Trischitta, "Teens Hospitalized After Smoking Mr. Nice Guy: State and Federal Governments Seek to Prohibit Legal Incense That Users Consider Fake Marijuana," *South Florida Sun Sentinel, http://articles.sun-sentinel.com/ 2011-01-05/ health/ fl-teen-legal-poy-20110105 _1_synthetic-marijuana-smoking-incense* (accessed August 31, 2011).
[2] Beth Rankin, "West Brook Student Hospitalized After Smoking Fake Marijuana," *Beaumont Enterprise,*

*http://www.beaumontenterprise.com/
news/article/West-Brook-
student- hospitalized-after-smoking-
730379.php*(accessed August 31, 2011).

[3] Alicia Fabbre, "County Tells Parents to Beware of Fake Marijuana," *Chicago Tribune,
http://articles.chicagotribune.com/ 2010-12-
22/news/ct-x-s-faux-marijuana -1222-
20101222_1_synthetic-marijuana-drug-court-
participants-fake-pot* (accessed August 31, 2011).

[4] *Willows Journal, http://www.willows-
journal.com/articles/ dea-5740-products-
chemicals.html* (accessed August 30, 2011); U.S. Department of Justice, Drug Enforcement Administration, "DEA Moves to Emergency Control Synthetic Marijuana," *http://www.justice.gov/dea/pubs/pressre
l/pr112410.html* (accessed August 30, 2011); and Donna Leinwand, "Places Race to Outlaw K2 'Spice' Drug," *USA Today, http://www.usatoday.com/
news/nation/2010-05-24-k2_N.htm* (accessed August 30, 2011).

[5] Ibid.

[6] Ibid.

[7] Sarah D. Wire, "Cops: Imitation Pot as Bad as the Real Thing," *Utah Standard-Examiner,
http://www.standard.net/topics/drugs/2010/02/17/
cops-imitation-pot-bad-real-thin* (accessed August 31, 2011).

[8] U.S. Department of Justice, Drug Enforcement Administration, "DEA Moves to Emergency Control Synthetic Marijuana."

[9] Melissa Jones, "Researchers Find Legal High More Potent Than Marijuana," *AFRO, http://www.afro.com/
sections/news/Baltimore/story.htm?
storyid=2341* (accessed August 31, 2011).

[10] John Gehringer, "K2 Ban Bill Moves to Senate," *The Maneater, http://www.themaneater.com/
stories/2010/3/5/k2-ban-bill-moves-senate/* (accessed August 31, 2011).

[11] Ibid.

[12] Katie Drummond, "Synthetic Marijuana Explained: Quick Facts About K2," *AOL News,* http://www.aolnews.com/2010/07/12/synthetic-marijuana-explained-quick-facts-about-k2/ (accessed August 31, 2011); and "Synthetic Marijuana Seized at Seven Calgary Stores," *Calgary Beacon,* http://www.calgarybeacon.com/2011/01/synthetic-marijuana-seized-at-seven-calgary-stores/ (accessed August 31, 2011).

[13] U.S. Department of Justice, Drug Enforcement Administration, "DEA Moves to Emergency Control Synthetic Marijuana."

[14] 21 U.S.C. §812 (13)(b)(1).

[15] Jessica Wehrman, "Fake Marijuana Spurs More Than 2,500 Calls to U.S. Poison Centers This Year Alone," American Association of Poison Control Centers, http://www.aapcc.org/dnn/Portals/0/K2rele asedec21.pdf(accessed August 31, 2011).

[16] Daina L. Wells and Carol A. Ott, "The 'New' Marijuana," *Annals of Pharmacotherapy* 45, no. 3 (2011): 414-417.

[17] National Council of State Legislatures, "Legislation on Synthetic Cannabinoids as of March 21, 2011,"http://www.ncsl.org/default.aspx?tabid=22431 (accessed August 31, 2011).

[18] Alan S. Zagier, "Bans on Fake Pot in 13 States Do Little to Deter Business," *New Orleans Times Picayune,* http://www.nola.com/crime/index.ssf/2010/09/bans_on_fake_pot_do_little_to.html (accessed on August 31, 2011).

[19] Jessica Wehrman, "Fake Marijuana Spurs More Than 2,500 Calls to U.S. Poison Centers This Year Alone."

[20] Katy Bergen, "Kansas Lab Looked at Synthetic Marijuana's Effect on Brain," *The Columbia Missourian,*http://www.columbiamissourian.com/storie s/2010/02/17/legal-substance-mimic-marijuana-has-harmful-effects/(accessed August 31, 2011).

[21] Ibid.

22 Sarah D. Wire, "Update: Toxicologists Studying Effects of Synthetic Pot," *The Columbia Missourian,http://www.columbiamissourian.com/ stories/2010/03/03/toxicologists-studying-effects-synthetic-pot/*(accessed August 31, 2011).

23 Jason Kuiper, "Busts Begin for K2 Possession," *Omaha World-Herald, http://www.omaha.com/ article/20110315/NEWS97/303159904/10* (accessed August 31, 2011).

24 David Vearrier and Kevin C. Osterhoudt, "A Teenager with Agitation: Higher Than She Should Have Climbed," *Pediatric Emergency Care* 26, no. 6 (2010): 462-465.

25 Ibid.

26 Keith Morris, "Synthetic Drug K2 Causes Overdose in Kanawha County, W.VA," *Charleston Environmental News Examiner, http://www.examiner.com/ environmental-news-in-charleston/ synthetic-drug-k2-causes-drug-overdose-kanawha-county-w-v* (accessed August 31, 2011).

27 Keegan Hamilton, "Daily RFT Product Testing Laboratory: K2 Synthetic Marijuana," *DailyRFT Blogs,**http://blogs.riverfronttimes.com/** dailyrft/201 0/02/daily_rft_product_testing_laboratory_k2_synthetic _marijuana _does_it_really_get_you_high.php* (accessed August 31, 2011).

28 Keegan Hamilton, "Daily RFT Product Testing Laboratory: K2 Synthetic Marijuana."

29 David Vearrier and Kevin C. Osterhoudt, "A Teenager with Agitation."

30 John Gramlich, "'Bath Salts' Pose New Test for Law Enforcement," *Stateline,http://www.stateline.or/live/d etails/story?contentId=548769* (accessed August 31, 2011).

DISCUSSION QUESTIONS

1. Should the public have to wait until the DEA places a "legal" substance in some sort of controlled substance schedule before law enforcement can effectively address the problem?

2. What might be some short term (tactical) or long-term (strategic) solutions to this dynamic problem?

CRITICAL THINKING EXERCISE

When I was a 21-year-old uniformed police officer, I often had young people pour their beer out and empty plastic baggies containing small amounts of marijuana they had in their possession for their personal use. I considered myself a "liberal" police officer, part of a new generation of cops. But within a couple of years I saw myself arresting—or issuing summonses for court appearances—to similar groups of people possessing these small quantities of alcohol and pot.

Why do you think this might have been the case? For this exercise, draw up of a list of potential reasons for a switch in enforcement methods. Feel free to agree or disagree with my methods.

Working Toward the Truth in Officer-Involved Shootings Memory, Stress, and Time

By Geoffrey P. Alpert, Ph.D,
John Rivera, and Leon Lott

May 2012: *FBI Law Enforcement Bulletin*

AN IMPORTANT AREA OF PSYCHOLOGICAL RESEARCH examines "how trauma and other highly emotional experiences can impact perception and memory."[1] Studies indicate that individuals display two distinct ways of processing information into memory: the "rational-thinking mode" during low-emotional states and the "experiential-thinking mode" in a high-stress situation, such as an officer-involved shooting (OIS).[2] This distinction illustrates that the trauma caused by an OIS likely will impact the memories and perceptions of the officers involved.

However, not enough research has been done to determine exactly how these effects distort memories of stressful events. Many studies relate only to routine memory and eyewitness identification, rather than the use of deadly force.[3] Further research must focus on determining how other variables may cause officers' memories of such incidents to vary from reality. Investigators who interview officers following an OIS should remain cautious because their subjects' memories may have been impacted by their experience in numerous and, at times, unpredictable ways.[4] Law enforcement agencies should acknowledge these difficulties when determining protocol for when and how to interview involved officers following an OIS.[5]

PRIOR RESEARCH

While much study has been conducted on memory and stress, only limited research has focused specifically on how this relates to OIS.[6] These gaps led one researcher to study how memories function differently during traumatic events. To investigate this issue, she surveyed officers over a 6-year period after they had been involved in shooting incidents. Her research found that officers exhibited a variety of reactions and responses to an OIS. For example, more than 60 percent of the officers felt that the incident transpired in slow motion, while 17 percent recalled time speeding up. Over 80 percent of the officers reported auditory lockout, while 16 percent heard intensified sounds.

Similarly, more than 70 percent claimed that they experienced heightened clarity of vision and that they responded to the threat not with "conscious thought," but, rather, on "autopilot." Interestingly, almost 40 percent reported disassociation, while 46 percent reported memory loss. Her findings are both important and consistent with other research indicating that officers experience perceptual and memory distortions during a critical incident, such as an OIS.[7]

Another study also deserves attention. Researchers surveyed 265 police officers from the Midwest who were exposed to three stressful conditions: a live-fire simulation, a video of the training that included the shooting, and a video of the simulation scene without sound or a shooting. Most of the officers were not questioned about their experiences until 12 weeks later, but a sample of the officers participated in a "rehearsal" interview—they answered the questions immediately after the exposure and then again 12 weeks later.

The researchers concluded that, overall, stress was positively related to memories of armed people, unrelated to memories of unarmed people, and negatively related to objects.[8] Their findings echoed other research that suggested eyewitnesses focus on the source of the threat or stress (e.g., the shooter) more intensely than the peripheral information about a scene or incident (e.g., the furniture in the room where the shooting occurred).[9] Interestingly, the study also found that the officers subjected to the immediate rehearsal questioning recalled clearer memories in their second interview 12 weeks later compared with the officers interviewed only once.

This study is important for several reasons. First, it showed that during high-stress events, officers more likely will focus on a threat, rather than peripheral objects or people. If an officer vividly remembers a person with a weapon but has only a blurred vision of an unarmed individual or an object in the room or area, this does not necessarily indicate that the officer's testimony is a conscious deception, planned response, or otherwise illegitimate.

Instead, these distortions may be caused by stress— the research indicated that officers' memories after a traumatic event can play tricks on them or vary from reality. This might result from pressure or anxiety caused by the incident, officers' exhaustion during the event, or other factors that influence memory.[10]

Second, the study supported the argument that it remains unclear as to when officers should be interviewed concerning their observations, actions, and reactions after an OIS. Many ambiguities exist regarding this issue, and, thus, no proven best practices exist for collecting information from officers involved in an OIS.

However, most agencies follow the intuition that exhausted, injured, or otherwise impaired officers should not be questioned immediately after a traumatic event. Otherwise, not only does this pose serious risks to the officers' health and well-being but information gleaned from these interviews may sabotage an investigation. These case studies indicated that through no fault of their own, these officers' memories may suffer from distortions due to the stress caused by such traumatic incidents. As such, investigators must keep these factors in mind when determining the timing and structure of post-OIS interviews.

AUTHORS' STUDY

To look at this phenomenon more closely, the authors organized a pilot study in December 2010 to examine how officers recall high-stress events. They used the Richland County, South Carolina, Sheriff's Department as the subject of their study. The researchers surveyed officers' reactions to training that involved live-fire simulation and role play by interviewing the officers and analyzing their responses.[11]

The department periodically conducts training activities that involve these live-fire simulations. This instance involved a group of deputies learning to respond to active-shooter situations in schools. The training occurred in an abandoned school that realistically emulated a real world environment. Officers responded to one of two active-shooter scenarios: a school shooting or a terrorist attack. Each simulation involved similar reportable and measurable characteristics.

During the simulation, officers worked in teams to clear a building, assist victims or hostages, and secure suspects. Following the incident, each deputy attended a short debriefing. When the training concluded for the day, half of the officers (Group A) wrote a report detailing the event. Then, the researchers asked Group A to recount the event again 3 days later. The other half of the officers (Group B) were required only to detail their recollections of the event after 3 days passed but were not asked to write a report immediately after the training.

By dividing the subjects into these two groups, the study aimed to determine whether officers' memories were sharper and more accurate in the time immediately following the shooting or sometime later. Also, Group A's rehearsal interview would help illustrate how their memories of a high-stress event changed over time.

Officers' memories were evaluated based on their ability to recall five elements of the event and the level of specificity that they provided. These five items were divided into two categories: threat variables and environmental variables. Each correct assessment of one of these elements earned officers a certain amount of points.

For threat variables, officers received 0 to 3 points for their descriptions of the number, type, and descriptions of weapons. An additional category of threat variables included information on the suspects, including race, gender, and clothing, earning officers another 0 to 4 points. Conversely, for environmental variables, officers earned 0 to 3 points for reporting the location of the incident, including the type of room and surroundings; 0 to 2 points for remembering facts from dispatch, including the nature of the altercation in progress; and another 0 to 2 points for reporting the number and names of other officers on the team.

Each report was assessed based on how accurately the officers could remember the five threat and environmental variables, and the deputies' scores in each category were summed to arrive at an overall score. Then, the total scores of all officers within the two groups were averaged.

FINDINGS

When officers in Group A detailed the event immediately after the simulation, their total score averaged 7.5 with a high score of 12 and a low score of 4 (out of 14 points possible). Three days later, when Group A's officers provided their recollections for the second time, their average score improved to 7.8 with a high score of 13 and a low score of 4. The total score for Group B's officers, who only provided their recollections 3 days after the simulation, averaged 6.4 with a high score of 10 and a low score of 2.

These results demonstrated that the deputies' memories remained sharper when asked to recount the incident immediately after it occurred, compared with the deputies who were not asked until a few days had passed. Additionally, the memories of individuals asked to share their recollections immediately after the incident improved slightly in their second report.

The researchers analyzed these results further by distinguishing officers' scores for threats versus environmental variables. A separate analysis of these scores (with a maximum score of 7 for each category) showed that the deputies recalled threats more accurately than environmental variables. Group A received an average score of 4.4 for threat variables compared with 3.3 for environmental variables.

Also, the results revealed that officers' recollections of threats weakened slightly over time as their score for threat variables decreased to 4.2. The subjects did not remember environmental variables as accurately in either condition. Group A showed an average score of 3.3 immediately after the event and 3.5 after 3 days passed. Group B averaged 3.3.

Although the differences were not drastic, they demonstrated that, overall, the deputies maintained stronger memories of threats (e.g., the people and weapons that could harm them), rather than the environment (i.e., the conditions under which the event occurred). Additionally, asking officers to recall facts immediately after an event may prove important for collecting accurate threat-related information because the officers' memories of threats weakened slightly after time passed.12 This could suggest that for investigators to obtain the most precise information about an OIS, it might be best for them to ask officers about threat-related information as soon as possible. Conversely, it may not be as urgent to interview witnesses about environmental variables right away.

Because this study involved a simulation, the subjects were not at risk for the same type of exhaustion, injury, or other impairments that can affect officers' memories after a real live-fire incident. But, the major lesson from this pilot study remains that these deputies recalled the threat variables better than environmental factors, and they remembered them best immediately after the incident.

POLICY IMPLICATIONS
Although a pilot study with significant limitations, this research presents important information for policy makers who determine whether an OIS investigation should involve immediate or delayed interviews of officers. Currently, no law enforcement-wide best practice or proven method exists for the timing of these interviews. However, several influential sources have suggested guidelines.

The Police Assessment Resource Center conducted a study of the Portland, Oregon, Bureau of Police and subsequently recommended that the department's internal affairs investigators interview officers who were involved in or witnessed an OIS no later than a few hours after the event.[13] Conversely, the International Association of Chiefs of Police stated in Police Psychological Services guidelines that investigators should give officers time to recover after the incident before they conduct any detailed interviewing, with this recovery time ranging from a few hours to overnight. Other experts echoed this recommendation; they suggested that officers may make more accurate and thorough statements if they are allowed to wait at least 24 hours before questioning, giving the officers time to rest and recuperate before they make a formal declaration.[14]

Many agencies embraced these suggestions and implemented policies requiring officers to wait before giving an interview or speaking to an investigator about an OIS. In this respect, these departments treat officers differently than they do suspects or civilian witnesses. If agencies think that officers involved in a traumatic event provide better accounts after a waiting period, then why are witnesses and suspects interviewed as soon as possible after the incident?

Prior research consistently determined that individuals' memories react strangely to stressful or traumatic events—officers and civilians alike experience perceptual and memory distortions after these incidents. What remains unknown, however, is what factors influence the distortions and how to minimize them.

To this end, it might be best for agency protocol to allow for case-by-case flexibility when determining the timing and structure of interviews following an OIS. Investigators must remain sensitive to personnel who have just experienced one of the most traumatic events in the life of a police officer but also strive to obtain the most accurate information possible about the incident.

For example, if investigators need precise intelligence about the incident, then it may be important for them to give the officers and civilian witnesses an initial walk-through of the incident without providing details. This walk-through may function as the "rehearsal" interview that helps trigger better memory recall later on as demonstrated in the authors' study. Similarly, an expert highlighted the value of this time delay in the interview process, stating that interviewers can consider "...providing enough brief information during an immediate on-scene 'walk-through' to get the investigation started."[15]

Also, investigators should remain sensitive to the fact that individual officers can react to an OIS differently. Some personnel handle the stress of a shooting better than others, and depending on the outcome of the event, it may be necessary to delay some detailed interviews. For example, if the officers' or witnesses' friends or family suffered injuries, investigators may need to delay asking them to rehash the incident in great detail.

Additionally, if individuals are exhausted, injured, or otherwise impaired, they will not provide meaningful information for any type of fact-finding mission. The decision of when to conduct post-OIS interviews should balance the humanistic concerns for the witnesses with the investigators' need for information.

Even officers employed by the same department and who received the same training may react differently to an OIS; as such, they could display varying levels of detail and accuracy in their recollections of the event. Officers' ages, backgrounds, and life experiences can impact significantly how they will respond to an OIS. Far too often, officers who suffer postshooting trauma feel further pressure from department administrators anxious for information.

This practice could be counterproductive because anything that causes the witness additional stress may hamper memory or recall. Putting pressure on officers by forcing them to recount a traumatic event too soon may result in incomplete and inaccurate information, possibly leading to grave errors in an investigation.

CONCLUSION

Clearly, more rigorous and precise research must focus on the factors that influence memory distortions and how to minimize them. Researchers have not reached a consensus on how to trigger more accurate memories of stressful events. Additionally, most investigators fail to anticipate the natural distortions, which likely occur due to expected variance rather than deception, that likely will appear in officers' memories. Until a greater understanding of these issues is reached, inconsistencies and inaccuracies in eyewitness testimonies will continue to hamper OIS investigations. Department leaders and personnel alike must acknowledge the many unpredictable factors that influence the memories of the involved officers after an OIS to ensure a successful investigation.

ENDNOTES

[1] Alexis A. Artwohl, "Perceptual and Memory Distortions in Officer-Involved Shootings," *FBI Law Enforcement Bulletin,* October 2002, 18-24.
[2] Seymour Epstein, "The Integration of the Cognitive and Psychodynamic Unconscious," *American Psychologist* 49, no. 8 (1994): 709-724.
[3] Terry Beehr, Lana Ivanitskaya, Katherine Glaser, Dmitry Erofeev, and Kris Canali, "Working in a Violent Environment: The Accuracy of Police Officers' Reports

About Shooting Incidents," *Journal of Occupational and Organizational Psychology* 77 (2004): 217-235.

4 David Hatch and Randy Dickson, *Officer-Involved Shootings and Use of Force: Practical Investigative Techniques* (Boca Raton, FL: CRC Press, 2007).

5 Nelson Cowan and Angela M. AuBuchon, "Short-Term Memory Loss Over Time Without Retroactive Stimulus Interference," *Psychonomic Bulletin Review* 15, no. 1 (2008): 230-235.

6 Matthew Sharpes, *Processing Under Pressure: Stress, Memory and Decision-Making in Law Enforcement* (Flushing, NY: Looseleaf Law Publications, 2009); *AELE Monthly Law Journal*, "Administrative Investigations of Police Shootings and Other Critical Incidents: Officer Statements and Use-of-Force Reports Part Two: The Basics," *http://www.aele.org/law/2008FPAUG/2008-8MLJ201.pdf* (accessed May 3, 2011).

7 Charles A. Morgan III, Gary Hazlett, Anthony Doran, Stephan Garrett, Gary Hoyt, Paul Thomas, Madelon Baranoski, and Steven M. Southwick, "Accuracy of Eyewitness Memory for Persons Encountered During Exposure to Highly Intense Stress," *International Journal of Law and Psychiatry* 27 (2004): 265-279; Alexis A. Artwohl and Loren W. Christensen, *Deadly Force Encounters: What Cops Need to Know to Mentally and Physically Prepare for and Survive a Gunfight* (Boulder, CO: Paladin Press, 1997); R.M. Solomon, "I Know I Must Have Shot, But I Can't Remember," *The Police Marksman,* July/August 1997, 48-51; R.M. Solomon and J.M. Horn, "Post-Shooting Traumatic Reactions: A Pilot Study" in *Psychological Services for Law Enforcement,* ed. J. T. Reese and H.A. Goldstein (Washington, D.C.: U.S. Government Printing Office, 1986), 383-394; D. Grossman and B.K. Siddle, *Critical Incident Amnesia: The Physiological Basis and the Implications of Memory Loss During Extreme Survival Situations* (Millstadt, IL: PPCT Management Systems, 1998); David Klinger, *Into the*

Kill Zone: A Cop's Eye View of Deadly Force (San Francisco, CA: Jossey-Bass, 2004); A.L. Honig and J. E. Roland, "Shots Fired: Officer Involved," *The Police Chief,* October 1998, 116-119; and Geoffrey Alpert, Dallas Police Department, *Review of Deadly Force Training and Policies of the Dallas Police Department* (Dallas, TX, 1987).

[8] Terry Beehr, Lana Ivanitskaya, Katherine Glaser, Dmitry Erofeev, and Kris Canali, "Working in a Violent Environment: The Accuracy of Police Officers' Reports About Shooting Incidents," *Journal of Occupational and Organizational Psychology* 77 (2004): 228.

[9] Cowan and AuBuchon, 230-235; David Frank Ross, J. Don Read, and Michael Toglia, ed., *Adult Eyewitness Testimony: Current Trends and Developments* (New York: Cambridge University Press, 1994); and Patricia Yuille and John Tollestrup, "A Model for the Diverse Effects of Emotion on Eye Witness Memory," in *The Handbook of Emotion and Memory: Research and Theory,* ed. S. A. Christianson (New Jersey: Lawrence Erlbaum Associates, 1992), 201-215.

[10] Marian Joëls and Tallie Z. Baram, "The Neuro-Symphony of Stress," *Nature Reviews Neuroscience* 10 (2009): 459-466.

[11] Deputies from numerous divisions in the department attended this training, and, as such, the researchers made no attempt to randomize the subjects or create a sample based on any factors. Additionally, no individual data were collected on the deputies' background or characteristics.

[12] No statistical significance tests were conducted because the purpose of this exercise was to examine the issues, rather than test for significant differences.

[13] Police Assessment Resource Center, *The Portland Police Bureau: Officer-Involved Shootings and In-Custody Deaths* (Los Angeles, CA, 2003).

[14] Grossman and Siddle, *Critical Incident Amnesia: The Physiological Basis and the Implications of Memory Loss During Extreme Survival Situations.*

[15] Artwohl, "Perceptual and Memory Distortions in Officer-Involved Shootings," 22.

DISCUSSION QUESTIONS

1. The authors ask a great question. For those agencies who believe a 24–48 hour time period should lapse before interviewing an officer in an OIS (for purposes of accuracy), why then do they interview victims and eyewitnesses immediately following the perpetration of the crime?

2. The authors suggest that perhaps one solution to the differences in opinion about when to interview an officer in an OIS, is to handle the matter on a case-by-case basis. What objective criteria (if any) might exist to assist in making such a determination on the spot?

CRITICAL THINKING EXERCISE

As a 25-year-old plainclothes police officer I violated one of the 10 Deadly Errors in law enforcement; I failed to recognize certain "danger signs." Consequently, a serial armed robber caught me off guard and held a large lock blade knife to my throat. But due to my training and experience as a street cop, I had the situation turned around in good order. Two shots took out the bandit who basically took a knife to a gunfight, but didn't know it. As I pulled my concealed snub-nose revolver, the sequence events began to go in slow motion. I definitely had tunnel vision—it was just me or him. I began to experience a mild degree of "detachment" once the threat was over and especially after overhearing an announcement on a police radio that the perpetrator was "DOA." *Based upon these facts, discuss among the team when you think would have been the best time for me to be interviewed by homicide detectives and/or internal affairs investigators, and support your decision by facts as best you can.*

Focus on Training
Training for Deadly Force Encounters

By Timothy Hoff

March 2012: *FBI Law Enforcement Bulletin*

FOR FIREARMS INSTRUCTORS, IT DOES NOT SUFFICE TO simply teach fellow law enforcement officers how to shoot. Each officer must master important fundamentals of marksmanship, such as grip, stance, sight picture, sight alignment, and trigger control. The duties of instructors include more than teaching students to hit a bull's-eye. Instructors must prepare them to survive deadly force encounters, or, in other words, to win a gunfight.

CHALLENGES

It is widely recognized that firearms qualification courses do not fully represent a real-world gunfight. Qualification courses measure officers' ability to apply the fundamentals of marksmanship, but with no one shooting back. Traditional flat-range drills help officers develop basic weapon handling skills, such as the draw and reloads, some of which also are tested during qualification courses. Mailboxes, automobiles, and other props can be positioned on the range to teach officers to seek and shoot from positions of cover and concealment. Reactive steel targets, especially dueling trees, can create safe, simulated "gunfights" in which two officers shoot against each other. These head-to-head competitions create stress by pushing the officers to shoot quickly and accurately.

Even more so than these tactics, shoot houses provide one of the best instruction tools to prepare officers for the threats they will encounter on duty. A shoot house allows instructors to teach law enforcement techniques, such as how to enter and clear rooms, hallways, and stairways, as well as team tactics. Shoot houses may be constructed to allow live-fire training with either simulated or actual duty weapons.

The walls of live-fire shoot houses may be built from used car tires filled with sand or ballistic steel walls covered with wood. Top-of-the-line shoot houses even offer moveable walls so the interior layout can be tailored to the mission. The more realistic the environment, the greater the training benefit. A shoot house proves valuable because it helps teach officers how to minimize risk to themselves during violent encounters. Officers learn tactics to clear rooms, hallways, and stairwells while decreasing their exposure to potential threats. They also build confidence by working as a team.

Unfortunately, high startup costs pose the biggest obstacle for developing shoot house training programs. Well-equipped shoot houses can be expensive, especially ones that incorporate multiple rooms, hallways, and stairs. The budget cuts and layoffs of today's economic climate make funding difficult. Additionally, local zoning ordinances can cause difficulties for departments seeking to build one of these facilities.

SOLUTIONS

Fortunately, the FBI's Detroit, Michigan, office identified a solution to develop a real-world tactical training program, even under these constraints. FBI Detroit does not possess its own shoot house; in fact, most FBI field offices do not own a dedicated house for conducting force-on-force or scenario-based tactical training. However, this did not prevent the agency from delivering high-quality, realistic training to its agents, as well as other officers. By partnering with the city of Dearborn, Michigan, FBI Detroit provides instruction for deadly force encounters for agents and task force officers, using residences complete with kitchens, bathrooms, stairs, and basements.

This program became possible when Dearborn's city government implemented a program to improve neighborhoods and maintain property values. As part of this initiative, the city purchased vacant properties, both single- and multifamily residences, in local neighborhoods, all of which had been marked for demolition. Some were allocated to local arson investigators to conduct burns for their own training programs.

FBI Detroit realized that if the fire department can burn down a house for training purposes, then, perhaps, one of these vacant properties could provide a safe place to conduct firearms training. Fortunately, the mayor's office, city council, and building department agreed, and they enthusiastically supported the FBI's request to use the city's property.

Clearly, a city-owned property presents some limitations. First, as the house is located in a residential neighborhood, instructors cannot incorporate exterior tactics into the training; during the program, instructors cover most of the windows to prevent outsiders from observing the techniques, tactics, and procedures. Second, the house is not located at or near the division's firearms range.

As such, the training cannot be conducted very frequently, whereas a dedicated shoot house would make it possible to incorporate high-quality tactical training into every firearms training session. Third, a dedicated shoot house would allow trainees to use actual duty weapons. However, given the cost savings and other benefits of using city-owned residences, they provide a viable option for live-fire training programs.

EQUIPMENT

In FBI Detroit's training program, officers and role players each are armed with realistic training weapons and ammunition. Role players carry guns that produce a loud realistic gunshot sound when they are fired; it is important for role players to fire a weapon that makes a loud noise so that if they surprise students in an ambush, the officers will respond to the sound of the blast. Students' guns closely resemble the look and feel of the standard-issue weapons for agents and task officers in FBI Detroit, which provides a significant benefit to the trainees.

TRAINING HOUSE

After securing the use of the two-story, single-family residence, instructors developed the curriculum and planned the actual training scenarios. The primary objective is to refine agents' ability to clear a location using the techniques that they learned at the academy. The house provides numerous opportunities for agents to practice these skills. To this end, this borrowed residence provides the additional benefit of more closely resembling the circumstances that agents will encounter on the job as most shoot houses only consist of one story and use simplified floor plans.

The instructors emphasize how to enter rooms properly and highlight the importance of visually clearing all areas prior to entry. Realistic photo targets and role players act as the officers' subjects during the scenarios. Professional support employees volunteer to serve as role players, but on most training days, only one or two role players are available. The photo targets supplement the role players, but they provide another advantage, as well—paper targets can be positioned in places where agents need to shoot at a close distance, such as just inside a doorway or closet.[1]

Trainers structure the exercises to position the agents for success. As such, they design every scenario so that agents successfully can complete the mission without firing any shots. The instructors strategically place the role players in spots where they anticipate the students might make mistakes; trainers instruct the role players to comply with the agents' commands, but not to react automatically. The students aim to locate the role players with proper clearing techniques, eliminating the need for an ambush. However, if the agents turn their backs on role players' locations or fail to clear the areas where role players hide, the role players can fire their guns to alert the agents to their mistakes.

STUDENT LESSONS

Many training groups use the appropriate tactics to successfully identify the role players, call them out of their hiding places, and secure them in a safe location, all without firing a shot. If an ambush occurs, the instructors quickly stop the scenario and discuss what mistakes led to the shooting. Then, the students reset and attempt to complete the scenario without firing their weapons. This structure illustrates that students can achieve the desired training results without firing a barrage of plastic bullets and BBs.

Of course, this program does not imply that officers never will be involved in shootings if they receive this training. Ultimately, the subject decides whether to peacefully comply with officers or fight them. Proper planning, such as ensuring superior manpower and firepower and using appropriate tactics, places maximum pressure on the subject to submit to the authority of law enforcement. Nonetheless, instructing officers on these techniques may help them avoid gunfire if possible.

Unlike typical shoot houses, the training house has bathrooms and a kitchen that agents have to clear. In several exercises, groups remembered to check the cabinets and other less obvious hiding places. However, a few groups ignored these danger areas despite reminders to clear all spaces large enough to conceal a two-legged threat. To emphasize this easy-to-overlook hiding place, one of the role players volunteered to hide inside a kitchen cabinet. It was a tight fit, but confirmed that this space was large enough to conceal a person. The role player waited until after the agents deemed the kitchen clear before emerging from the cabinet and opening fire on several trainees. Those agents who were shot, even with a simulated gun that caused them no harm, learned a valuable lesson and likely never will clear a kitchen the same way again.

INSTRUCTOR LEARNING
Not all the lessons have been learned by the students; the instructors have acquired valuable knowledge as well. One important lesson came during an exercise in which a role player hid in a hallway closet. The subject did not have a weapon, so he was not in a position to be shot. When a student opened the door and saw the role player, he was so surprised that he literally jumped.

Witnessing the trainee's automatic reaction reminded the instructors about the importance of mental preparation and proper mind-set. Initially, the instructors focused on the mechanics of law enforcement clears, but from that rotation on, instructors stressed to students the mental importance of remaining alert to threats hiding in every cabinet, closet, or corner. The eyes see what the mind expects.

SAFETY PRECAUTIONS

During these exercises, safety remains of the utmost importance. In the same week that FBI Detroit conducted training, an officer in another state died during a similar training exercise. The news reports indicated that a fellow officer wanted to demonstrate a technique to his colleagues during a break.

Unfortunately, the officer performing the demonstration unknowingly picked up a live-fire weapon instead of a training gun, and he shot and killed his fellow officer. To prevent such tragic events from occurring, the lead instructor or a dedicated safety officer must prevent any ammunition or live-fire weapons from entering the training environment. Normally, officers learn never to point their weapon at another person unless the situation warrants it (e.g., for self-defense).

However, these training sessions differ from standard law enforcement environments because students and role players are not only allowed but expected to point their weapons at another person to complete the scenario. As such, students, role players, and instructors alike must realize the significant risk that accompanies pointing a weapon of any sort at another person, even during a training exercise.

To increase safety even further, the FBI adopted a color-coding system for weapons. For example, guns marked with red are inert—the firing pin has been removed and the barrels have been plugged so that they cannot fire, but they are functional in every other respect. Orange designates simulated guns, which fire plastic marking rounds. The vendor who supplies these weapons agreed to apply orange paint to the slides and magazine floor plate for a minimal fee. This color-coding scheme reduces the likelihood of potentially tragic mistakes.

At the conclusion of training, it is the instructors' responsibility to make sure that officers return to duty with fully loaded, live-fire weapons. Incidents have occurred when students went back on patrol with training weapons still in their holsters. Fortunately, the color-coded weapons make it readily apparent when an officer does not have the proper equipment.

RESULTS
It still is too early to fully measure the success of this training effort. The real test will be whether or not the program makes FBI Detroit's agents and task force officers safer while they perform their duties, and that test does not end until the student retires. However, the course evaluation forms were overwhelmingly positive. The most common recommendation for improvement was to hold this type of training more often, which, in itself, indicates some level of success.

CONCLUSION
FBI Detroit's program demonstrates a strong example of how law enforcement agencies can deliver high-quality tactical instruction for deadly force encounters, even if they do not have sufficient funds to build a dedicated shoot house. Using city-owned residences provides a budget-friendly, effective way to deliver firearms training in a realistic environment.

No one location or facility will allow for training activities that encompass every potential situation that law enforcement officers will face. Ideally, agencies can establish dedicated shoot houses or 180-degree shooting bays for officers to practice room entries with live fire. However, even if an agency has its own shoot house available, the use of commercial and residential buildings marked for demolition provides a low-cost way to develop realistic force-on-force training programs.

ENDNOTES

[1] To ensure safety, agents should not fire a training gun at a role player without at least 3 feet of distance or else risk injury.

DISCUSSION QUESTION

1. When considering training for deadly force encounters, do you think the FBI should train its own agents or would the agents be better served by receiving training from members of the Detroit Police Department who face such events practically on a daily basis?

CRITICAL THINKING EXERCISE

The author correctly points out that it is too early to draw any conclusions as to the success of this program. If you were selected to evaluate this program, what steps would you take in carrying out such an undertaking? Be sure to include research methods in your evaluation plan.

RESTRAINT IN THE USE OF DEADLY FORCE
A PRELIMINARY STUDY

By Anthony J. Pinizzotto, Ph.D.,
Edward F. Davis, M.A., Shannon B. Bohrer, M.B.A.,
and Benjamin J. Infanti, M.A.

June 2012: *FBI Law Enforcement Bulletin*

O CCASIONALLY, NEWS ARTICLES AND TELEVISION reports bear banner headlines claiming a general and widespread use of excessive force by America's law enforcement officers.[1] Some radio commentators and citizens participating in call-in programs claim to know of an increase in such incidents. Further, scholarly articles have addressed the issue.[2] And, in fact documented cases do exist of officers using excessive, even deadly, force. However, is this presumption of widespread force overstated?

The authors do not intend to justify or even attempt to explain away any use of excessive force in law enforcement. Excessive—specifically, unnecessary, unwarranted, and disproportionate—force is both unlawful and unethical and has no place in the American justice system. Rather, the authors intend to reflect their discussions with thousands of police officers throughout the country over the past 30 years while teaching, conducting research, and engaging in consultations on various cases regarding the use of force—to include deadly force—in law enforcement.[3] In some instances, officers used force; in others, they had it used against them, at times resulting in serious injuries and even deaths. In addition to speaking to the officers who took part in situations involving force, the authors also interviewed many of the suspects and offenders in these cases.

The authors' experiences have revealed that a large number of officers have been in multiple situations in which they could have used deadly force, but resolved the incident without doing so and while avoiding serious injury. This led to an important issue. The authors know how many individuals officers justifiably kill each year (on average, approximately 385).[4]

However, the authors do not have even an estimate of the number of times officers legally and ethically could have used deadly force but did not. Therefore, they will discuss preliminary data regarding the issue of restraint in the use of deadly force within the law enforcement profession.

THE DEADLY MIX

The authors conducted their original research on law enforcement safety while active members of the FBI, assigned either at its headquarters in Washington, D.C., or at the FBI Academy's Firearms Training Unit or Behavioral Science Unit in Quantico, Virginia.[5] This research resulted in three publications.

The first, *Killed in the Line of Duty*, in 1992, was a national study that examined 51 incidents in which an officer was feloniously killed in the line of duty.[6] The second study, *In the Line of Fire*, in 1997, examined 40 incidents of serious assaults on law enforcement officers.[7] In 2006, the final publication, *Violent Encounters*, expanded the scope of the first two studies and focused on specific topical issues regarding the use of force in law enforcement.[8]

Each study within this law enforcement safety trilogy, as well as subsequent articles the authors wrote using data from these studies, focused on some aspect of what they termed "the deadly mix"—that is, the dynamic interaction of the officer, the offender, and the circumstances that brought them together.[9]

Any encounter where an officer was assaulted or killed transpired in a dynamic, evolving scene that included the perceptions of the officer and the offender. As they interacted, both persons altered these perceptions and the concomitant interpretations. And, based on those assessments of one another's behaviors, each acted accordingly.

At that moment, the fluid movement of the deadly mix—set in motion when the offender and officer came together—began to shift. All of this occurs within only seconds, but has life-altering consequences. This concept of the deadly mix might shed light on the circumstances in which officers, although legally and ethically justified to use deadly force, did not.

CASE EXAMPLES

The following real-life scenarios can be considered in two ways: 1) as examples of the dynamic and fluid movement of the deadly mix and 2) as a possible model for examining apparently similar situations in which some officers are killed and others are not.

In the first case example, the offender was arrested for feloniously killing a law enforcement officer during a traffic stop. When the authors interviewed this subject, he claimed that another officer stopped him in a similar traffic incident 1 week prior to the killing. Similarities and differences in these two cases *in the mind of the offender* are significant to the authors' discussion of the deadly mix.

In the first incident, the traffic stop took place at night. The offender had committed an armed robbery earlier that evening and did not know whether the officer had notified the dispatcher prior to the stop. When the officer activated the emergency lights, the subject knew that if he waited for two more blocks to pull over, he would come to a darker area with fewer streetlights.

So, he continued to drive in spite of the officer now engaging the siren. When the offender finally pulled over, he saw "that the officer was looking directly at me and was talking on the radio at that point. I had a gun under the front seat of the car, but I knew he was watching me, so I didn't move."

As the officer exited his vehicle, the offender noticed that he "had his hand on his gun." The offender explained, "I knew that he could pull his gun faster than I could get to mine...so I decided to wait and see what was going to happen." The officer told the subject to "remain in the car and keep your hands on the steering wheel." This was said "in a voice that I knew he meant what he said."

The officer asked the offender why he did not pull over immediately, and the subject said that he "didn't know you wanted me to pull over." The officer told him that he stopped him because his left brake light did not work. After the offender produced a valid driver's permit and registration, the officer simply told him to "have that light fixed" and returned to his police vehicle.

When the authors questioned the subject, he stated that he felt the officer was in complete charge of the incident. The offender believed that if he "had gone for my gun, he would have killed me. And that wasn't worth it...even if it meant going to jail."

The subject described himself as a predator and claimed that he "was looking for an opportunity to assault the officer who stopped" him. What did the officer do or not do that prevented an assault? The traffic offense that the officer acted on—a broken left brake light—was minor, but the officer never reduced his awareness of anything that might happen when making the stop. As the offender stopped his vehicle, he saw the officer watching him while talking on the radio. Although this officer notified the dispatcher of the stop, he did not become distracted from observing the actions of the driver.

As the officer exited the patrol vehicle, he continued to watch the subject. He placed his hand on his weapon while approaching the stopped car. The officer strengthened his position of authority by immediately issuing a command to "remain in the car and keep your hands on the steering wheel." The manner and voice inflection used by the officer convinced the driver to look for an easier victim and not try to retrieve his gun from under the seat, even if it meant going to jail that night.

The second incident involving this offender, which resulted in the death of an officer, also occurred during a traffic stop at night. The subject had reported a history of carrying concealed weapons throughout his adolescent and adult life. He also had a past arrest for using a firearm in the commission of a crime and had served time in prison.

An officer operating radar pulled him over for speeding. At the time of the traffic stop, the subject was transporting marijuana and cocaine in amounts that would have resulted in an arrest and a possible felony conviction. In addition, a warrant had been issued for him due to a parole violation. As soon as the officer engaged the emergency lights, the offender pulled to the side of the roadway. Believing that the officer was aware of the warrant, the offender thought, "If they catch me with drugs, I'm in for a long time."

As he looked in his rearview mirror, he "saw the officer get his hat on and pick up something from the seat and get out of the car...but he wasn't watching me." While continuing to observe the officer, the offender simultaneously took his own weapon from under the car seat and prepared to shoot the officer as he approached his vehicle. In the offender's words, "I believed I could get him before he knew I had a gun." His assessment proved accurate.

The victim officer in this case had made several traffic stops for excessive speed while operating radar. In each instance, he issued a traffic citation and released the driver without incident. The offender, who exceeded the speed limit by 12 miles per hour, drove by the officer. When the officer activated the emergency lights, the offender immediately pulled to the side of the road and stopped.

Did the officer reduce his level of awareness because of the appearance of immediate compliance? No one ever will know. The offender intently watched the officer and noticed that he not only did not use his radio but was not closely watching him. Therefore, the subject removed his gun from under the seat.

The offender saw the officer pick up something from the seat, exit the patrol vehicle, and walk toward his car. During the approach, the subject noticed that the officer continued not to look at him. The offender acted on his observations and lowered the driver's side window.

As the officer arrived at the window, the offender shot and killed him before he could make any statement to the driver. The object the subject saw the officer pick up from the seat was a ticket book. Responding officers found the victim's service weapon in his holster when they arrived at the scene.

APPLICATION AND ANALYSIS

The two case examples involved traffic stops made at night on the same offender. In each incident, the offender assessed both the circumstances of the stop and the behaviors of the officers.

Was the offender accurate in his assessment of the two officers in these traffic stops? In the authors' past articles, they continually reported that officers might do everything they were trained to do in a situation, yet possibly be feloniously killed.[10]

The circumstances at the scene of these traffic stops varied by location, lighting, and traffic; each of these factors had an impact on the offender's decision to assault or not. Use of alcohol or other drugs during a particular incident also can affect offenders' ability to make an accurate assessment.

Killed in the Line of Duty featured the following statement:

Overall, it is clearly an oversimplification to say one error or mistake caused a law enforcement officer's death. Some of the killers in the study appear to have *evaluated a series of actions or inactions of the officer before considering an assault on the officer* [emphasis added].[11]

In the two case examples, the same offender considered both actions and inactions of the officers before deciding what to do. This discussion does not suggest that in the second of the two cases the officer was killed because he made a mistake. Rather, consistent with the theory of the deadly mix, an examination of this incident suggests that the death resulted from a confluence of several factors, to include the perceptions and behaviors of the officer, the perceptions and behaviors of the offender, and the circumstances that brought the two together.

The feloniously killed officer had stopped a number of cars that night without incident. As other officers related, he only sporadically advised the dispatcher of the cars he pulled over depending on the number and frequency of his stops, as well as availability of radio traffic. He had effected an arrest earlier in the evening for a DUI without incident.

However, in this case, he was unaware of the outstanding warrant on the driver, the offender's possession of drugs, and the presence and availability of the weapon. Additionally, the subject stated that he "was sure I could get away with this" because the officer "didn't look like he was paying any attention to what I was doing."

The results of the three studies on law enforcement safety have been applied to various areas of law enforcement training, supervision, and investigation. Specific topics include suicide by cop; the role of perception of both the officer and the offender, to include memory and recall; implications for interviewing officers and offenders in use-of-force situations; personality aspects of offenders; postassault trauma; encounters with a drawn gun; searches; off-duty performance; backup; protective body armor; and mind-sets of officers and offenders.

USE OF RESTRAINT

The concept of the deadly mix—with its emphasis on the dynamic interaction of the officer, the offender, and the circumstances that brought them together— can provide insight into restraint in the use of deadly force. An example of an officer encountering two subjects in a traffic stop combines the principles of the deadly mix with the officer's ability to read and react to a dynamic set of circumstances that, in turn, influences the decision as to the use of deadly force.

Descriptive Statistics of the Survey Sample				
Survey Item	n	M	SD	Total
Years in LE	295	17.0	8.3	5017
Firearms Drawn/Year	271	66.3	110.5	17977
Critical Incidents	235	20.0	49.9	4696
Deadly Force Incidents				
Fired	293	0.3	0.7	87
Did Not Fire	282	3.9	13.7	1102
Assaults	287	7.1	15.7	2030
Injuries				
Accident	295	0.8	1.6	228
Assault	294	0.5	1.0	136
LE = Law Enforcement n = Number of Participants M = Mean SD = Standard Deviation				
Deadly force incidents indicate critical encounters where deadly force was a legal option.				

A state patrol officer in a marked cruiser patrolled an interstate highway and witnessed a vehicle changing lanes without caution. After a short pace, the officer determined that the vehicle was going faster than the posted speed limit, so he activated his emergency lights. The officer observed the driver, along with a passenger who appeared to be slouched in the right front seat. The vehicle did not stop immediately, but continued until it subsequently pulled to the side of the roadway and came to a halt. The officer noticed that this was an area of dim lighting.

The officer immediately called in the traffic stop by location and vehicle license plate number. He approached the vehicle from the rear of the driver's side with his flashlight in his weak hand. Thinking that he had a drunk driver, the officer stopped at the center post and looked inside the car.

The male passenger was slumped in the seat as if sleeping, and the driver's window was down. The officer demanded the license, registration, and proof of insurance from the female driver. As she fumbled in her purse, the officer saw the man slide his hand under the driver's leg and grab a gun. The officer immediately dropped to the ground and retreated to the rear of the car. He called for backup and reported the presence of the firearm.

The man with the gun turned from side to side, but could not locate the officer, who continued to command the subjects to remain in the car and drop the weapon. When backup arrived, officers removed the two subjects from the car without incident and retrieved the gun from the right floorboard of the vehicle. The male later stated that he "would have shot at the officer, but never had a clean shot."

The officer may have acted with additional caution after the driver failed to immediately stop. He took control of the situation by the placement of his patrol vehicle and the heightened attention he gave when approaching the subjects' vehicle. The message he transmitted by voice and behavior was clearly received by the pair in the car. They understood that he was ready and able to react to whatever they might attempt.

In this case, the officer would have had legal and ethical justification to use deadly force. The offender not only produced a weapon but later admitted in the interview that he would have shot the officer if he "could have gotten a clear shot." However, the officer believed that he safely and successfully could control the occupants of the car without the use of deadly force.

TRAINING AND RESEARCH

In 2010, the U.S. Department of Justice, Bureau of Justice Assistance, awarded a grant to the authors and to the Fairfax County, Virginia, Police Department to educate the law enforcement community regarding the principles of the deadly mix.[12] The training was designed and implemented as a 1-day session for state, municipal, and local law enforcement instructors and followed a train-the-trainers format.

Ten sites from across the nation were selected, and the training was offered to approximately 50 students at each site. The participants were exposed to the principles of the deadly mix and their application to officer safety, supervision, and the investigation of the use of force. Students received hard copies of the trilogy on law enforcement safety, a CD with electronic copies of each study, and contact information for obtaining additional copies of each study for their own trainees. Each participant also received a CD that contained the computer-based presentations, video clips used in the course of victim officers and offenders, and lesson plans for each presentation.

Student Survey

During the training, participants completed a confidential survey questionnaire regarding their own use of force, as well as some related issues. The questions dealt with the 1) number of years in law enforcement, 2) average number of times the officers drew their firearms per year, 3) number of critical incidents in which they were involved, 4) number of critical incidents in which they fired their weapons, 5) number of times during their career in which they legally could have discharged their firearm in the performance of duty (shooting at someone) but chose not to fire, 6) number of times they had been assaulted during their careers, 7) number of times they were injured that required time off due to accidents, and 8) number of times they had been injured due to an assault that required them to take time off because of the injury. A total of 295 law enforcement officers participated in the survey questionnaire. These participants had an average of 17 years of law enforcement experience.

Results

Table 1 contains general descriptive statistics for the survey sample's questionnaire.[13] These include the number of participants scored for each question, the mean for each question, the standard deviations of the means, and the total number of incidents for each question. What follows is a description of the results relevant to the discussion of the use of deadly force and restraint.

Two hundred sixty participants (96 percent) responded that they drew their firearms at least once each year. These officers believed they acted under threatening or critical circumstances.

One hundred ninety-seven participants (83 percent) responded that they had been involved in at least one critical incident during their careers. Fifty-nine participants (20 percent) indicated that they had been involved in at least one critical incident where they fired their weapon. Conversely, 197 participants (70 percent) responded that they had been involved in at least one situation where they legally could have discharged their firearm in the performance of their duties but chose not to fire. This corresponds with the information reported in *Violent Encounters* where 36 of the 50 officers stated that they legally could have discharged their firearm in the performance of duty.

Two hundred twenty-eight participants (80 percent) responded that they had been assaulted at least once during their career. Seventy-eight participants (27 percent) responded that they had received an injury due to an assault that required time off from duty.

DISCUSSION

The results of the study indicated that 80 percent of the officers had been assaulted during their career and that officers were assaulted an average of approximately seven times in the line of duty. Most assault data on law enforcement officers are highly conservative because most officers do not report being assaulted. Officers either believe that being assaulted "comes with the job," or their idea of an assault is when they receive injuries requiring medical treatment.

The study found that approximately 70 percent of the sample of police officers had been in a situation where they legally could have fired their weapon during a critical incident but chose not to. Officers were involved in an average of four such incidents during the course of their career. Only 20 percent of the sample had been involved in critical incidents where they fired their weapon during the incident.

These results are pertinent in the discussion of restraint by law enforcement officers and their decision to use deadly force. Officers in the sample were involved in a total of 1,102 situations where they could have fired their weapon legally and ethically as defined by both law and by the organizational regulations of the respective police departments, but did not. The 87 total incidents in which officers legally fired their weapon during critical incidents pale in comparison with the number of situations where they chose not to fire.

Officers in the sample were involved in 1,189 situations where deadly force was a legal course of action. Officers used deadly force in 7 percent of these situations. In other words, officers in the sample used restraint 93 percent of the time even when not legally mandated to do so. This percentage represents a significant amount of restraint by police officers. Further, in accepting the conservative nature of the data analysis, officers most likely used restraint in deadly force more often than what is accounted for in the data.

If officers risk their personal safety by using restraint in deadly force, why has this phenomenon largely gone unnoticed in the media and research? An analysis of research on the topic of deadly force yields no studies directly related to the use of restraint in deadly force by agents of law enforcement. Instead, many studies have focused on environmental characteristics of situations where law enforcement officers used deadly force.[14] Research efforts also have examined how organizational factors influence deadly force.[15]

Taken together, these studies found that organizational factors, such as departmental policy, can curtail and somewhat control the use of deadly force.[16] However, these efforts did not assess the perceptions, beliefs, and thought processes of the individual officer in the situation. Studies that have taken this approach in research on deadly force focused on the perceptual distortions and psychological aftereffects of officers involved in deadly force situations.[17] Thus, the body of research on deadly force has failed to examine the impact of the individual officer's thought processes in the decision to use deadly force or restraint.

In regard to the media, cases involving deadly force overshadow the actuality that police officers overwhelmingly employ restraint in their use of deadly force. Perhaps, this media focus on the use of deadly force helps create the misconception that police officers use deadly force more often than they actually do. As the results of this preliminary study indicated, this is not the case.

Another important consideration in the discussion of deadly force is accuracy. A police officer's decision to use deadly force in choosing to fire during a critical incident does not guarantee success. One researcher noted that police officers miss targets more often than they hit them when using deadly force.[18] Further, hitting the target does not indicate whether a suspect was killed. Thus, the present study's finding that there were 87 incidents where an officer used deadly force does not equate to 87 lethal shootings. Although somewhat simplistic, this reasoning is essential in conceptualizing the use of deadly force.

LIMITATIONS OF THE STUDY

The most noteworthy limitation of the present study is that it was a preliminary exploration into the use of restraint in deadly force. Although research on deadly force has been conducted since the 1970s, a study on restraint in deadly force is a relatively new concept.[19] As such, the fact that this study was preliminary does not diminish its significance. Instead, it was meant to establish a basis for future research on the topic.

Another limitation is that the concept of restraint cannot be further defined based on the present results because the questionnaire did not delve into the inner psychology and perceptions of police officers in their decision to use restraint with deadly force. Once again, this is attributed to the preliminary nature of the data.

A final limitation of the study is the self-reported information from the sample of police officers. The possibility exists that the self-reported data from the questionnaires are not representative of the actual phenomenon of restraint. Further, the responses given by the police officers in the study cannot be validated by objective reports on the careers of each individual officer. Nevertheless, the questionnaire responses are assumed to be reliable and valid. Additionally, as open-ended, nonnumerical answers to the survey were excluded, 85 responses were not considered in the analysis of the data; this exclusion likely led to conservative results.

FUTURE DIRECTIONS IN RESEARCH

The findings of this study as they relate to restraint in deadly force have significant implications for future research in the field. For example, what factors led to the officers using restraint? Does the use of deadly force reduce or increase the inclination of officers to use restraint in subsequent critical incidents? How do individual officers perceive restraint and deadly force? What characteristics of a critical incident lead to deadly force?

These questions highlight the importance of the deadly mix in systematically studying and understanding restraint in deadly force. The core components of the deadly mix represent the dynamic nature of any law enforcement situation where the officer, offender, and circumstances come together. The decision to use deadly force is made in an instant. The factors that come together in the mind of the officer to use or not use deadly force can change dramatically within an individual encounter.

The fluid nature of this deadly mix can help examine the officer's decision to shoot or not shoot within that given set of rapidly changing circumstances. Further research on restraint can elucidate how these three factors influence an officer's decision to use deadly force in the line of duty. The results of these studies can assist administrators, supervisors, investigators, officers involved in deadly force encounters, other officers from the department, prosecutors, citizens, and the media to better understand and evaluate the use of force in law enforcement.

From a training standpoint, an additional avenue of future research is the applicability of restraint in situations of excessive force. As stated earlier, excessive force—specifically, force that is unnecessary, unwarranted, and disproportionate—is both unlawful and unethical. Therefore, it is essential that research analyzes how restraint can safeguard against the excessive use of force. These principles then can be applied to officer training in safety and tactics.

CONCLUSION

This preliminary examination of restraint in the use of deadly force established the extent to which a sample number of police officers used restraint throughout their careers. A survey on the use of force found that police officers exercised restraint in deadly force in 93 percent of the situations where they legally could have fired their weapons. This finding sharply contrasts with the public perception of police officers and the use of deadly force.

Documented research on restraint currently is lacking. There were two related issues under which the data found in this article were collected. First, the authors recognized that there exists an idea, created in part by the media, within society that there is excessive and widespread use of deadly force within the law enforcement community. Second, against this social perception, the authors wished to assess the view within a portion of the law enforcement community regarding how they see law enforcement's use of deadly force. The results of this preliminary review show dramatic differences between the two groups.

Future research is needed that reveals confirmed and validated numbers where law enforcement officers could have used deadly force, but refrained from doing so. Agencies that currently record instances regarding the circumstances where officers have drawn their firearms without firing them can assist in this important research question.

Conceptualizing restraint in terms of the theory of the deadly mix reveals the dynamic nature of restraint in deadly force. In doing so, law enforcement entities can ensure the safety of the officer, the public, and the offender while maintaining order and justice.

ENDNOTES
[1] K. Johnson, "Police Brutality Cases on Rise Since 9/11," *USA TODAY,http://www.usatoday.com/news/nation/2007-12-17-Copmisconduct_N.htm* (accessed June 23, 2011); S. Lendman, "Police Brutality in America," *Baltimore Chronicle &*

Sentinel,http://baltimorechronicle.com/2010/071310L endman.shtml (accessed June 23, 2011);
and *RTAmerica*, "Police Brutality Increases in U.S.," *http://www.youtube.com/watch?v=TalvTj-vmLw* (accessed June 23, 2011).

[2] H. Cooper, L. Moore, S. Gruskin, and N. Krieger, "Characterizing Perceived Police Violence: Implications for Public Health," *American Journal of Public Health* 94 (2004): 1109-1118.

[3] Dr. Pinizzotto, Mr. Davis, and Mr. Bohrer.

[4] U.S. Department of Justice, Federal Bureau of Investigation, *Crime in the United States, 2009,http://www2.fbi.gov/ucr/cius2009/offenses/expanded_information/data/shrtable_14.htm* (accessed June 23, 2010).

[5] Dr. Pinizzotto and Mr. Davis.

[6] A.J. Pinizzotto and E.F. Davis, U.S. Department of Justice, Federal Bureau of Investigation, *Killed in the Line of Duty: A Study of Selected Felonious Killings of Law Enforcement Officers* (Washington, DC, 1992).

[7] A.J. Pinizzotto, E.F. Davis, and C.E. Miller III, U.S. Department of Justice, Federal Bureau of Investigation,*In the Line of Fire: Violence Against Law Enforcement* (Washington, DC, 1997).

[8] A.J. Pinizzotto, E.F. Davis, and C.E. Miller III, U.S. Department of Justice, Federal Bureau of Investigation,*Violent Encounters: A Study of Felonious Assaults on Our Nation's Law Enforcement Officers*(Washington, DC, 2006).

[9] A.J. Pinizzotto and E.F. Davis, "Interviewing Methods: A Specialized Approach is Needed When Investigating Police Deaths," *Law and Order* 44, no. 11 (1996): 68-72; A.J. Pinizzotto and E.F. Davis, "Suicide by Cop: Implications for Law Enforcement Management," *Law and Order* 47, no. 12 (1999): 95-98; A.J. Pinizzotto and E.F. Davis, "Offenders' Perceptual Shorthand: What Messages are Law Enforcement Officers Sending to Offenders?" *FBI Law Enforcement Bulletin,* June 1999, 1-6; A.J. Pinizzotto, E.F. Davis, and C.E. Miller III, "Suicide By Cop:

Defining a Devastating Dilemma," *FBI Law Enforcement Bulletin,* February 2005, 8-20; A.J. Pinizzotto, E.F. Davis, and C.E. Miller III, "The Deadly Mix: Officers, Offenders, and the Circumstances that Bring Them Together," *FBI Law Enforcement Bulletin,* January 2007, 1-10; and A.J. Pinizzotto, E.F. Davis, S.B. Bohrer, and R. Cheney, "Law Enforcement Perspective on the Use of Force: Hands-On, Experiential Training for Prosecuting Attorneys," *FBI Law Enforcement Bulletin,* April 2009, 16-21.

[10] A.J. Pinizzotto and E.F. Davis, "Cop Killers and Their Victims," *FBI Law Enforcement Bulletin,* December 1992, 9-11; and A.J. Pinizzotto, and E.F. Davis, "Killed in the Line of Duty: Procedural and Training Issues," *FBI Law Enforcement Bulletin,* March 1995, 1-6.

[11] Pinizzotto and Davis, "Killed in the Line of Duty," 48.

[12] U.S. Department of Justice, Bureau of Justice Assistance, National Initiatives: Enhancing Law Enforcement (Category V - National Officer Safety Training and Technical Assistance).

[13] For data quality and reliability, the authors took into account only numerical responses, disregarding questions answered with words, such as "multiple," "many," or "several," as well as those left blank or answered with "unknown." Overall, out of a possible 2,360 responses, 85 were disqualified. Another discrepancy concerned an error in which 42 participants did not have the question about the number of critical incidents involved in throughout their careers. Although this slightly limited the utility of the data pertaining to that question, the authors believed that the 42 possible answers did not exert significant influence over the results. Further, this error does not affect the reported results or subsequent discussion on restraint in the use of deadly force. An additional consideration involved the way in which the authors coded 49 responses with a

"+" at the end of the reported numerical answer. For example, they coded a response of "25+" as "25." This coding technique yielded conservative results.

[14] J.P. McElvain and A.J. Kposowa, "Police Officer Characteristics and the Likelihood of Using Deadly Force," *Criminal Justice and Behavior* 35 (2008): 505-521.

[15] H. Lee and M.S. Vaughn, "Organizational Factors That Contribute to Police Deadly Force Liability,"*Journal of Criminal Justice* 38 (2010): 193-206; A.N. Tennenbaum, "The Influence of the Garner Decision on Police Use of Deadly Force," *Journal of Criminal Law & Criminology* 85 (1994): 241-260; M.D. White, "Controlling Police Decisions to Use Deadly Force: Reexamining the Importance of Administrative Policy,"*Crime & Delinquency* 47 (2001): 131-151; and M.D. White, "Examining the Impact of External Influences on Police Use of Deadly Force Over Time," *Evaluation Review* 27 (2003): 50-78.

[16] S.E. Wolfe and A.R. Piquero, "Organizational Justice and Police Misconduct," *Criminal Justice and Behavior* 38 (2011): 332-353.

[17] N. Addis and C. Stephens, "An Evaluation of Police Debriefing Programme: Outcomes for Police Officers Five Years After a Police Shooting," *International Journal of Police Science and Management* 10 (2008): 361-373; A. Artwohl, "Perceptual and Memory Distortion During Officer-Involved Shootings," *FBI Law Enforcement Bulletin,* October 2002, 18-24; and D. Klinger, "Police Responses to Officer-Involved Shootings," *National Institute of Justice Journal* 253 (2006): 21-24.

[18] M.D. White, "Hitting the Target (Or Not): Comparing Characteristics of Fatal, Injurious, and Noninjurious Police Shootings," *Police Quarterly* 9 (2006): 303-330.

[19] McElvain and Kposowa, "Police Officer Characteristics and the Likelihood of Using Deadly Force," 505-521.

DISCUSSION QUESTIONS

1. What other possible inferences or conclusions might be drawn from the study based upon the fact that officers used restraint in deadly force situations in at least 93 percent of the time?

2. According to this article, the public has a perception of rising incidences of unauthorized use of deadly force. Do you think that the results of this study should be widely disseminated to the public in order to counter such an unsupported notion? Why or why not?

CRITICAL THINKING EXERCISE

I have analyzed the results of these excellent FBI studies many times. They provide some very useful information that is mostly based upon common sense, but which has also been corroborated through interviews with officers and offenders. Your assignment is to identify five factors that contributed to the officers' survival and five that might be attributed to their injuries or deaths. To do this, draw upon information provided in this article as well as from Pierce Brooks' 1976 bestseller *Officer Down, Code Three* (Motorola Teleprograms), which was standard issue when I attended the police academy in 1978. Another great reference book that many of my partners and I used is *The Tactical Edge: Surviving High-Risk Patrol* by Charles Remsberg (Calibre Press).

EMERGENCY VEHICLE SAFETY
By Thomas J. Connelly

February 2012: *FBI Law Enforcement Bulletin*

WHETHER IN A LARGE METROPOLITAN AREA OR IN A quiet rural setting, police officers performing patrol functions do not simply use their patrol cars to transport them from call to call, chase down a traffic violator, or patrol their assigned areas; they also use their vehicle as their personal office. Like typical offices, the police vehicle is equipped with pens, paper, note pads, a computer, a radio, a telephone, and the forms necessary to complete reports and other paperwork. As in any other office setting, police officers use their vehicle to conduct meetings and interviews. Sometimes, officers even drink their coffee and eat their lunch in the car, just like most of us who work in a traditional office. Thus, patrol cars not only serve numerous functions but present many distractions.

In my years in law enforcement, I found that 25 to 30 percent of police officer line-of-duty deaths resulted from motor vehicle traffic collisions.[1] Officers sustain many more nonfatal injuries each year as a result of traffic collisions involving patrol cars. Also, many line-of-duty deaths result from violent acts that occur in or within close proximity to the officer's vehicle.

When officers drive at high speeds through a densely populated area, they may not only endanger themselves but also, perhaps, the public. This situation is exacerbated by officers' inherent stress and distractions when responding to a high-risk, life and death situation. The public expects police officers to assume these risks at all times, under all conditions, without exposing those around them to an unreasonable level of elevated danger. Police executives and administrators expect the same.

IN-CAR TECHNOLOGY
Consider the equipment installed in a police vehicle to make an officer's job safer and easier, including technology, such as computers, video cameras, license plate readers, two-way radios (sometimes more than one), stolen-vehicle locator devices, and manually operated light and siren controllers. Can these pieces of equipment create a distraction to the officer when operating their car? In my experience, they do.

When I was driving a patrol car, I found myself trying to multitask and operate a computer that could access various law enforcement databases and send messages to other cars or the dispatcher. I cannot say the number of times that I looked up from the keyboard just in time to avoid sideswiping a parked car or rear-ending a stopped one! Fortunately for me, I never was involved in a collision due to my attention being diverted while typing in a license plate number or messaging another officer. I was lucky, but others have not been as fortunate. Most agencies' policies and procedures prohibit operation of the computer while driving. It is a practice that officers on the road should avoid.

I also was involved in a number of high-speed pursuits during my career. Although most police officers are excellent multi-taskers, it is difficult to drive a patrol car at high speeds during a pursuit while operating the lights and siren and talking on the radio to fellow officers and the dispatcher. Add inclement weather or maneuvering through a school zone with children present, and it is easy to see the intense physical stress officers face. High-speed pursuits probably are the most dangerous situations threatening the safety of officers as well as the public. Though officers reasonably must pursue violent offenders to keep their communities safe, the public expects them to keep citizens' safety interests in mind while engaged in high-speed pursuits.

As technology has developed, especially in the mobile policing environment, it increasingly has become integrated into the police vehicle. Thirty years ago, the typical police car was equipped with a two-way radio and a controller (possibly a set of toggle switches) for the lights and siren, usually mounted below the dashboard, somewhat out of the way. In contrast, many police cars today have several two-way radio systems, a light and siren controller, a computer, a video system with cameras mounted on the ceiling of the car and a separate monitor to review videos, license plate readers, moving radar transmitters, stolen-vehicle locator systems, and other mission-critical systems.

ERGONOMICS
With all of this technology in police cars, it is a wonder that officers wearing 12-pound utility belts, a sidearm, and body armor will fit inside! Also, consider that the new 2012 police vehicle models from major manufacturers will be somewhat smaller inside than the vehicles prominently in use today. Significant injury avoidance in vehicle ergonomics is becoming a real consideration for police executives and risk managers.

Ergonomics represents a risk management concern in most industries today. Many employers, including law enforcement agencies, are required to develop and adopt a comprehensive injury and illness prevention plan (IIPP) in their work environments. Workplace ergonomics plays a significant part in any IIPP. The cost to businesses of repetitive stress injuries (e.g., back injuries, carpal tunnel syndrome, persistent migraines) due to poor ergonomics is significant. Police executives and risk managers need to consider not only the direct costs of medical care related to ergonomic injuries but also the indirect costs associated with reduced productivity, increased absenteeism, and damaged employer-employee relationships when evaluating the impact of ergonomic injuries.

Organizational leaders and risk managers proactively identify potential hazards and conditions that could lead to unnecessary injuries in the workplace and strive to enhance workplace safety. Do the guidelines and standards set forth in an organization's IIPP carry over to officers' patrol cars? If they do not, should they? A concerted effort to make the inside of the patrol car as ergonomic as possible will reduce the impact of repetitive stress injuries and avoidable driver distractions related to routine police vehicle operations.

DISTRACTIONS BEHIND THE WHEEL
Distracted driving is another factor to consider in reducing the injuries and fatalities associated with police vehicle operations. Police officers perform myriad tasks behind the wheel. Concurrently, they must safely operate their vehicles at all times in the communities they serve. And, the more activity going on in the police car, the more likely the police officer driving the vehicle will be distracted. Officers are

trained to handle distractions and should be assessed periodically on how well they do so.

SAFETY STEPS
Multiple approaches exist that can enhance the safety of emergency vehicle operations and reduce the number of preventable injuries and deaths that result from those operations. These approaches include evaluating alternative vehicle technology systems for safety, periodically reviewing emergency vehicle operations training programs, critically reviewing of policies and procedures related to emergency vehicle operations continually, implementing tracking systems for on-duty collisions (especially avoidable ones), integrating innovative vehicle safety technologies, and considering the potential negative safety impacts created before new technologies are integrated into existing emergency vehicle systems.

UPDATED TECHNOLOGY
Several actions can help address some of the concerns related to the technological systems currently integrated into the standard patrol car. Most of that technology is stand-alone. With multiple radio control heads, monitors, keyboards, cameras, and radar control units inside the passenger compartment, it seems that the integration of these systems in police vehicles, perhaps, requires further consideration, especially from a safety and ergonomics perspective.

Many patrol cars today appear cramped and cluttered. As a result, law enforcement agencies and technology-product vendors in the public sector must develop ways to integrate the various systems in police cars to eliminate any disordered appearance. In addition, development of an intuitive, user-friendly operating system for the integrated technology is paramount. I have seen several systems currently marketed to law enforcement agencies that attempt to integrate the various technological and operational controls, reportedly enhancing the safety of patrol cars as a result.

I have seen only one integration system that eliminates the clutter of control heads and redundant monitors in the vehicle and incorporates a selection of control methods. This system integrates the radios, light and siren controllers, moving radar control heads, video control heads, and other external technologies into the mobile computer, which offers control via several easy-to-use methods.

The first method incorporates a hand-controlled device mounted on the floorboard between the seats. Drivers can operate the lights, siren, and radios with one hand without having to divert their attention away from the roadway. The second method involves voice commands. Most of the system's functions can be controlled by simple voice commands, including queries of license plates and people, thereby eliminating the need to type on the keyboard while driving. The final method employs a touch-screen user interface. By using a system, such as this, the radios, light and siren controllers, video controllers, and other clutter-causing equipment are removed from the passenger compartment of the police car and mounted remotely, typically in the trunk. This allows vehicles to appear roomy, neat, well-designed, and airbag compliant.

Vehicle Operations Training

In addition to systems upgrades, police administrators should review their basic emergency vehicle operations training programs. In this regard, a number of critical issues require consideration: how frequently training is held, number of hours committed, if that time commitment is adequate, whether the training mirrors realistic situations, and if reviews of current policies and procedures are included as an integral part of the training.

Modifying or expanding vehicle operations is a sensitive issue, especially considering the financial constraints that local law enforcement agencies face today. However, there may be creative ways to enhance this training without a significant budget impact. Roll-call training, shared regional instruction, and video training serve as examples of less expensive, yet viable methods. Agencies need to be creative in this area. Police executives and training coordinators could refer to various industry-specific resources to help them develop innovative training programs. Some of these resources include the Police Executive Research Forum (PERF), the International Law Enforcement Educators and Trainers Association (ILEETA), various private universities and research organizations, and local or regional training academies.

Policy Development and Enforcement
Another necessary step involves ongoing critical review of department policies and procedures specifically related to emergency vehicle operations and pursuit driving. Ensuring compliance with contemporary laws and legal mandates related to emergency vehicle operations is crucial. Addressing activities that can lead to distracted driving (e.g., typing license plate numbers or messages into the computer) also is an important consideration. Ensuring compliance with these policies through consistent disciplinary intervention is imperative, not only when accidents occur but whenever a violation of policy is detected. In doing so, the policy is given credence throughout the organization.

A number of resources are available to assist police executives with policy review and development. The International Association of Chiefs of Police is a useful resource providing access to sample policies and topic-specific research. PERF and other state and regional police chiefs' organizations are great resources as well. Private companies also provide policy development services to police agencies for a subscription fee, though some risk management groups will pay subscription fees for law enforcement organizations.

Tracking and administratively reviewing all on-duty traffic collisions is another useful approach related to policy development and enforcement. If an employee is involved in a number of avoidable collisions at a rate higher than the norm, the officer's driving record merits further investigation. Determining the root causes of collisions and developing plans to address those, whether individually or organizationally, is important. Sometimes, additional training specifically developed for the officer, in addition to any other required in-service training, is appropriate.

Other times, formal discipline resulting from identified policy violations might be necessary. Occasionally, the officer may not have the skills required to operate a patrol vehicle and its mobile technology safely, which could necessitate elevated levels of disciplinary intervention. The systematic review of emergency vehicle collision reports and employees' driving records also may help identify the need for a change of organizational policy or training.

The impact of adapting to new technology in police cars is another important consideration for police executives and managers. Technology continues to evolve, and, as it does, new products will be incorporated into the mobile policing environment. When these technologies are adopted, the impact that their presence and operation will have on the driver must be considered. Then, through the steps described previously, any potential increased risk factors can be adequately addressed and mitigated before the technology is implemented.

NEW SAFETY SYSTEMS

A greater number of cars today have higher-level safety systems built into them at the factory. These systems further can enhance safety in the mobile policing environment. Some new vehicles are equipped with proximity-warning devices that sound an alarm when objects get too close to them. Others have automatic lane-drift warning systems and automatic braking in case the vehicle is approaching another car or an object and is not slowing down or braking. Some even have pre-collision impact systems that activate built-in safety systems before a collision occurs, while others can parallel park on their own. Police administrators and fleet managers can work with vehicle manufacturers to ensure that they integrate as many safety features into police fleet vehicles as they can.

CONCLUSION

Since the introduction of new and multiple technologies into police vehicles over the past few decades, the resulting clutter, driver distractions, and ergonomic degradation of the passenger compartment has created a situation wherein safe vehicle operation may have been sacrificed.

To halt this trend, a multifaceted approach is required. Integration of new and innovative technologies, from space-saving computer systems to emerging vehicle safety features, is imperative for officers behind the wheel. At the same time, the development of contemporary policies and procedures related to emergency vehicle operations, with consistent enforcement and requisite training, are important for officers when not on the road. These all are options that police department executives and administrators must heed to enhance officer safety and minimize the number of police injuries and deaths attributable to on-duty traffic collisions.

ENDNOTES

[1] The author derived this percentage from his professional experience and expertise.

DISCUSSION QUESTIONS

1. If you had to write a policy on emergency vehicle safety (but not dealing with when or when not to engage in pursuits, which are covered below), *what key areas do you think should be covered?*

2. Officers have been convicted of reckless driving and even manslaughter in instances involving motor vehicle accidents. Such events often result from the officer proceeding through a red light or a stop sign even though emergency lights and sirens had been activated. *What do you think the law should be on this subject?*

CRITICAL THINKING EXERCISE

My first day out of the police academy and on the street was a great experience. My field training officer (FTO) let me take the wheel, and sometime after midnight I engaged in my first high speed chase after four teenagers who had escaped from a juvenile correctional facility and had stolen the car. I still recall my FTO, who was working the radio, advising the communications center they we were at speeds over 120 MPH. If we had a pursuit policy at the time, I wasn't aware of it. *In outline form, list as many factors as you can that you feel should be addressed in such a policy, and be prepared to discuss your reasons for including them.*

EVIDENCE-BASED DECISIONS ON POLICE PURSUITS
THE OFFICER'S PERSPECTIVE
By
David P. Schultz, Ed Hudak,
and Geoffrey P. Alpert, Ph.D.

March 2010: *FBI Law Enforcement Bulletin*

"**P**ERHAPS THE MOST COMPELLING, ONGOING, AND logical reason for law enforcement's continued interest in high-speed vehicle pursuits has been its concern in balancing the values of crime control and offender apprehension with ensuring the safety of all parties who potentially might be involved—police officers, suspects, victims, bystanders, and the community."[1] This balancing test has formed the cornerstone of pursuit policies, training, and practice for the past several decades.

Police pursuit records provide some frightening statistics. First, the majority of police pursuits involve a stop for a traffic violation. Second, one person dies every day as a result of a police pursuit. On average, from 1994 through 1998, one law enforcement officer was killed every 11 weeks in a pursuit, and 1 percent of all U.S. law enforcement officers who died in the line of duty lost their lives in vehicle pursuits. Innocent third parties who just happened to be in the way constitute 42 percent of persons killed or injured in police pursuits. Further, 1 out of every 100 high-speed pursuits results in a fatality.[2]

Within the context of these horrific statistics, officers are charged with protecting public safety, which often requires serious personal and social risks. Although empirical evidence is scant, each study conducted on police pursuits enhances the available knowledge. That is the main purpose of the authors' research, along with providing policy makers and trainers another tool to assist them in formulating evidence-based decisions.[3]

DYNAMICS OF PURSUITS

Obviously, the goal of the officer is to apprehend and arrest the suspect. While the officer originates an enforcement stop, the suspect, if he flees, initiates a pursuit.[4] When this occurs, the officer must respond to the suspect—who has no rules—with a balanced and reasonable approach to apprehend him. Accordingly, the officer must become aware of personal capabilities and take into account environmental conditions that may affect his ability to accomplish the overall mission of the police, to protect lives.

The officer must factor into the decision-making process the risk created by the suspect's driving, the potential actions of innocent bystanders and others who may become involved, and the influence of his actions on the suspect's driving. In addition, the officer must consider the likelihood of apprehension in the decision to continue a chase. In other words, the officer must balance the goals of law enforcement with the public's safety.

The officer must understand that when a suspect refuses to stop for the emergency lights and siren, a common encounter turns quickly into a high-risk and dangerous event where the "show of authority" may negatively affect the suspect's driving. If the suspect continues or increases his reckless operation of the vehicle, the officer, basing his reaction on policy and training, must respond to the potential benefit and risk of the pursuit and also understand the influence of the chase on the participants.

The need to "win" and make that arrest can be influenced by the adrenaline rush felt by the officer who also must recognize that the fleeing suspect will have the same experience. Because research has demonstrated the impact of this on an officer's vision, hearing, motor skills, and decision making, it would appear necessary to prepare for the same adverse affect it could have on fleeing suspects.[5]

Clearly, a pursuit is an exciting event and involves one person running to escape and another chasing to catch. One important challenge for the officer is that there are only limited ways to get the suspect to stop, including a tire deflation devise, a precision immobilization technique (PIT) maneuver at proper speeds and locations, or an application of deadly force.[6]

The dynamics of most pursuits include the fleeing suspect raising risks to the welfare of the officer, the public, and himself by not stopping and then driving recklessly. The fleeing suspect is attempting to escape the consequences of his actions and avoid being taken into custody. Most pursuits are for minor offenses, and whether those fleeing suspects have committed a serious crime is pure speculation.[7] In addition, research has shown that if the police refrain from chasing all offenders or terminate their pursuits, no significant increase in the number of suspects who flee would occur.[8]

One of the dilemmas faced by law enforcement is whether or not to continue a chase. Stated differently, the question is, What are the consequences of continuing or terminating a dangerous pursuit? Most policies include the balanced and reasonable approach and require officers to terminate when the risks created by the chase outweigh the need to immediately apprehend. It is understood that when an officer terminates his active involvement in a pursuit, the suspect likely will escape apprehension at that time.

Many progressive policies instruct officers who terminate a chase to stop, pull over, radio their position, and drive away from the suspect to signal that the officer has given up and the suspect has "won." The point of this tactic is to notify dispatch of the termination and to inform the suspect that he can slow down and drive safely without constantly looking in his mirrors. The question is, When will the suspect slow and his driving become safe? Without a doubt, the reckless actions of the fleeing suspect can create a dangerous situation for all concerned. The question of when the suspect will slow down and return to reasonable and safe driving, however, remains.

INSIGHT FROM SUSPECTS

Because knowledge of suspects' behavior is limited to anecdotal information from officers and empirical data from the suspects themselves, four researchers conducted a study as part of a grant from the National Institute of Justice wherein they interviewed suspects who had fled from the police.[9] Their effort, the first systematic study to quantify the perceptions of suspects involved in pursuits, provided information on a variety of topics, including the demographics of those who fled from the police (their average age was 26, and 94 percent were male), as well as what happened (30 percent of the suspects crashed, 30 percent stopped, and 25 percent outran the police) and why they fled (32 percent were driving a stolen car, 27 percent had a suspended driver's license, 27 percent wanted to avoid arrest, and 21 percent were driving under the influence).[10]

One of the more interesting findings from the suspects concerned their willingness to slow down when the police stopped chasing them. Approximately 75 percent reported that they would slow down when they felt safe. They explained that on average, they would have "to be free from the police show of authority by emergency lights or siren for approximately two blocks in town...and 2.5 miles on a freeway."[11] In other words, suspects who have fled from the police report that once the officer terminates the pursuit, they will slow down within a reasonable period.

In addition to the suspects' data on pursuit termination, a researcher surveyed members of the Airborne Law Enforcement Association to determine their experiences with pursuits. The data revealed that after ground units terminated their pursuit, "on average, suspects continued driving dangerously for 90 seconds before slowing."[12] The researcher concluded that "results from this pilot study, other prior research, and anecdotal evidence suggest most fleeing suspects will return to safe driving behavior within a relatively short period of time after ground pursuits are terminated. However, there will be those cases where despite law enforcement efforts to pursue less frequently and to terminate more pursuits as quickly as possible, fleeing suspects will create tragedies."[13]

During years of training officers in decision making, instructors have heard a wide array of responses concerning the behavior of fleeing suspects during pursuits. The anecdotal information has indicated that officers realize suspects will not continue their recklessness forever and at some point will slow down. Conventional wisdom has suspects reducing speed quickly in town and after a longer period on a highway or freeway. Discussions of officers' beliefs about the behavior of fleeing suspects have been neither extensive nor systematic; they have occurred during training, debriefings, and in other informal situations.

While the research has been scant, the opinions about suspect behavior have been widespread. Discussions held in training sessions point to a wide variety of opinions concerning pursuits, the proper police response, and suspect behavior. What is known is that pursuits are dangerous and place officers, citizens, and suspects at risk. What is not known is how to make them safer for all concerned. Some policies mandate the termination of a pursuit when the risks outweigh the benefits. The thinking behind this approach is to have the police not be part of the problem but part of the solution.

If possible, a safe and proper PIT maneuver can bring an end to some chases. In many other cases, it is more appropriate for the officer in a pursuit to turn off his lights and siren and stop or turn around. This behavior is designed to signal to the suspect that he is safe and can slow down and remove the risk to the public. Once the suspect receives this signal, it is anticipated that he will slow down. As in any aspect of law enforcement, defensible decisions should be based on empirical evidence. In pursuit matters, however, suspects have claimed that they will slow down and become safer relatively quickly after a pursuit is terminated. But, what do officers have to say about these issues?

No attempt has occurred to quantify officers' experiences or perceptions about the behavior of fleeing suspects. The authors' study, therefore, complements the research conducted with suspects by asking police officers many of the same questions.

PERCEPTIONS OF OFFICERS

Starting in July 2007 and ending in June 2008, the lead author surveyed participants in the Law Enforcement In-Service Training in Emergency Vehicle Operations and Police Pursuits course at the Minnesota Highway Safety and Research Center in St. Cloud. He collected data from 1,015 officers, representing 10,968 years of experience. Agency size ranged from two to 1,624 sworn officers, with the average being 40. Data also were collected from 362 preservice recruits who attended training during the same period.

Obviously, this method of data collection relies on memory and perception. It is important to recognize that any self-reported data may have errors of memory and maturation. However, when requesting information that is neither sensitive nor consequential, it is likely that respondents will provide honest answers. The researchers gave the officers and recruits sufficient time and instructed them to report their information as accurately as possible. A few officers and recruits did not answer some questions, but the missing answers were minimal.

The officers reported being involved in a total of 10,384 pursuits of which 959 (9 percent) resulted in a collision involving a police vehicle and 3,571 (34 percent) ended with the suspect crashing. While some involved multiple objects, the authors estimated that 35 to 40 percent of all of the pursuits resulted in a crash. These officers terminated 1,133 (11 percent) of their pursuits with 447 of those involving motorcycles. The officers advised that they believed 227 (20 percent) of the pursuits they terminated resulted in a crash. In addition to halting pursuits by turning off the emergency lights and siren, they used the PIT maneuver 1,018 times that resulted in 35 (.03 percent) injuries and no deaths, demonstrating that the PIT can be effective and efficient when used properly.

The preservice recruits reported that they believed that 61 percent of the pursuits would end in a crash and that if they terminated a pursuit, 39 percent of those would crash anyway. In other words, these young recruits believed that by terminating the pursuit, 22 percent fewer crashes would occur.

TABLE I. OFFICERS' PERCEPTIONS OF FLEEING SUSPECTS' BEHAVIOR

	In-Town Pursuits	Out-of-Town Pursuits	70% of Officers*
Number	985	983	684
Missing	30	32	
Mean	1.72 blocks	7 miles	3.9 miles
Median	1	5	5
*Officers who reported on average that suspects would quit running after 10 miles.			

Perhaps the most important aspect of this research involved the officers' and recruits' opinions concerning when a fleeing suspect would slow down after a chase had been terminated. The authors asked the officers and recruits, "If a pursuit was terminated, how far do you believe the suspect would run if in town and if out of town?" Table 1 shows the answers for in-town pursuits in blocks and for those conducted out of town in miles and tenths of a mile.

On average, the officers reported that suspects would quit running after 1.7 blocks in town. Overall, 98 percent advised that suspects would stop within five or fewer blocks. The other two percent believed that the suspects would continue fleeing for a greater distance.

In out-of-town pursuits, the officers thought that on average, suspects would quit running after seven miles. Seventy percent believed that suspects would stop within 10 miles, whereas 30 percent felt that the suspects would continue beyond that distance. The officers who believed that suspects would quit running before 10 miles reported an average response of slightly less than four miles. That is, those officers who believed that suspects would be impacted by their lights and sirens being turned off felt that suspects would quit running after 3.9 miles.

Similarly, 62 percent of the officers indicated that suspects would quit running within five or fewer miles with an average response of 3.5 miles. Interestingly, the recruits—who had no real experience with policing or pursuits—advised that fleeing suspects would quit running after 2.9 blocks in town and 4.2 miles out of town. Overall, the authors interpreted these findings to indicate that most officers generally believe suspects will quit running after about two blocks in town and approximately four miles out of town.

IMPLICATIONS OF RESEARCH
Balancing the need to immediately apprehend a fleeing suspect with the risk created by the chase forms the foundation of police pursuit policies. The operational meaning of this test is that once an officer terminates his pursuit, the suspect will slow down and blend into traffic, go home, or exit the vehicle and try to escape on foot. In other words, pursuit policies are based on the notion that once an officer or supervisor terminates a pursuit because the risks are too great, the public will be safer than if the pursuit is continued. Unfortunately, empirical research on the actions of fleeing suspects is scarce, but the data in this study expressed officers' opinions on what suspects will do after they terminate their active attempt to apprehend such individuals.

Evidence-based decision making in law enforcement has been an important improvement in policy development and training.[14] As researchers and police agencies form partnerships and conduct collaborative studies, the results can be used to design best practices and evaluate practitioners. As a result, both the law enforcement community and the public will benefit from decisions based on systematic research findings. Additionally, policies and training can be explained to officers using quantitative and qualitative research findings as opposed to anecdotes.

CONCLUSION

While more research needs to be conducted on the actions of fleeing suspects after a pursuit has been terminated, it is noteworthy that fleeing suspects and officers have provided similar answers to the questions of suspect behavior. Specifically, the majority of suspects reported that they would slow after two blocks in an urban area, while the officers thought the suspects would do so in just under two blocks.

On freeways, the majority of the suspects reported that they would slow after 2.5 miles, whereas most of the officers felt they would after just under four miles. Because the reality may be somewhere in between these estimates, more research is needed to test these findings. While the research reported here or anywhere else cannot predict the actions of a specific suspect, it does suggest that in the aggregate, fleeing suspects will behave within specified parameters.[15]

It is important to consider that pursuit policies are based on the belief that fleeing suspects will slow down at some point after a pursuit is terminated. Research findings support that principle and provide empirical data that can guide policies and training. Of course, whether or not police officers should terminate an active attempt to apprehend a suspect is a different question that depends on what they know or have reasonable suspicion to believe that the suspect has done.

ENDNOTES

[1] C.M. Lum and G. Fachner, *Police Pursuits in an Age of Innovation and Reform* (Alexandria, VA: International Association of Chiefs of Police, 2008), 4.

[2] John Hill, "High-Speed Police Pursuits: Dangers, Dynamics, and Risk Reduction," *FBI Law Enforcement Bulletin*, July 2002, 14-18.

[3] The authors presented findings from their initial research on this topic in "Emergency Driving and Pursuits: The Officer's Perspective," *FBI Law Enforcement Bulletin*, April 2009, 1-7. The current article includes additional research they have conducted since then.

[4] For clarity and illustrative purposes, the authors refer to officers and suspects as males.

[5] James Meyerhoff, William Norris, George Saviolakis, Terry Wollert, Bob Burge, Valerie Atkins, and Charles Spielberger, "Evaluating Performance of Law Enforcement Personnel During a Stressful Training Scenario,"*Annals of the New York Academy of Sciences* 1032 (2004): 250-253.

[6] G. Alpert, D. Kenney, R. Dunham, and W. Smith, *Police Pursuits: What We Know* (Washington, DC: Police Executive Research Forum, 2000).

[7] John Hill, "High-Speed Police Pursuits: Dangers, Dynamics, and Risk Reduction."

[8] For a discussion of the experiences of the Orlando, Florida, Police Department, see G. Alpert, R. Dunham, and M. Stroshine, *Policing: Continuity and Change* (Long Grove, IL: Waveland Press, 2006), 194-205.

[9] R. Dunham, G. Alpert, D. Kenney, and P. Cromwell, "High Speed Pursuit: The Offender's Perspective,"*Criminal Justice and Behavior* 20 (1998): 30-45.

[10] Suspects could list more than one reason.
[11] Dunham, Alpert, Kenney, and Cromwell, "High Speed Pursuit: The Offender's Perspective," 38.
[12] Jeff Martin, "Pursuit Termination: A Lifesaver?" *Law and Order* 49 (2001): 30-33.
[13] Ibid.
[14] L. Sherman, *Evidence-Based Policing: Ideas in American Policing* (Washington, DC: Police Foundation, 1998).
[15] This would be an ecological fallacy.

DISCUSSION QUESTION

It is true that most pursuits were initiated by drivers who refused to stop after the officer observed a relatively minor motor vehicle violation. However, in many instances, the drivers had committed more serious violations or crimes, which results in the paradoxical situation where the officer believes he or she is making a traffic stop for the motor vehicle violation and the driver may believe that he is being pulled over for the more serious crime. With all of the horrible statistics concerning deaths of officers and innocent citizens, there are many groups that call for an end to pursuits for minor traffic violations. *What is your view on this?*

CRITICAL THINKING EXERCISE

I chased a car one summer night that I had observed travelling the wrong way on a one-way street without its headlights on. Soon, with my lights and siren activated, the driver and occupants were throwing items out of the car. Once at a dead end in a parking lot, the driver spun around, and pointed a handgun at me. I ducked below the steering wheel, drew my firearm, and heard him drive away. I was eventually back on his trail, but as the gunman sped through a number of red lights, and I slowed down before proceeding through the intersections, I lost him. Eventually a 9-11 call came in reporting that a car had crashed through a fence and into a citizen's back yard. Approximately 10 minutes later, another 9-11 call came in from the registered owner of the vehicle reporting that his car had been stolen. *Critique my actions up to the point of the 9-11 calls, and describe what you would have done thereafter.*

Campus Safety
Assessing and Managing Threats

By Mario Scalora, Ph.D.; Andre Simons, M.A.; and
Shawn VanSlyke, J.D.

February 2010: *FBI Law Enforcement Bulletin*

CAMPUS PROFESSIONALS MUST ASSESS THE RISK POSED by known individuals, as well as by anonymous writers of threatening communications. The authors offer threat assessment and management strategies to address the increased demands faced by campus law enforcement, mental health, and administration officials who assess and manage threats, perhaps several simultaneously.[1]

A CHALLENGE

Campus police departments have come under increasing pressure to address targeted violence and related threatening activity. College and university grounds often are porous, vulnerable to various types of threats (e.g., stalking, domestic violence, and other activities conducted by disturbed or disgruntled students and employees) from both internal and external sources.

The campus safety professional must deal both reactively and proactively with these numerous threats. As much of the current literature concerning campus violence has focused on the elementary and high school levels, campus safety officials often must rely on data and research related to a younger age demographic operating in less diverse physical environments.

Campus law enforcement and safety agencies often are small compared with urban police departments, yet they operate within large, active communities. Further, campus safety officials must work with a variety of stakeholders, including faculty, staff, administrators, students, and community members, and coordinate with law enforcement agencies responsible for the overall jurisdiction within which the institution is located.

The campus safety official must accomplish all of this while preserving the tenets of an academic environment that values debate, free expression, and creativity. Unfortunately, the effort may be complicated by the fact that some people view law enforcement through an adversarial lens where campus safety measures conflict with these academic ideals.

A SOURCE OF HELP

Through the application of case experience, education, specialized training, and research, the FBI's National Center for the Analysis of Violent Crime (NCAVC), part of the Critical Incident Response Group (CIRG), provides behaviorally based investigative and operational support to complex and time-sensitive situations involving violent acts or threats. Its Behavioral Analysis Unit-1 (BAU-1) assesses the risk of potential terrorist acts, school shootings, arsons, bombings, cyber attacks, and other incidents of targeted violence. Since April 2007, the unit has responded to numerous college and university requests to address cases of potential mass shooters. However, BAU-1 also has worked cooperatively with campus safety officials to craft effective threat management strategies pertaining to many other types of campus-oriented threats.

- For 20 years, a male subject with no formal relationship to or status on a campus but residing nearby continually harassed students and staff and blatantly disregarded formal requests to stay away from the grounds. Recently, he sent a letter containing hyperreligious references and veiled threats to the administration in which he expressed outrage over the revealing nature of dress exhibited by coeds attending services at his church.

- Extremists targeted a university laboratory because of its use of animals in research. Officials became concerned that one or more insiders set up the attack and continued to pose a threat to the safety of the laboratory, campus, and staff. University professors engaged in biomedical research received death threats, including those targeting their family members, at their residences.

- College authorities received a frantic call from a parent of an incoming freshman who had found a profile on a social networking website of his assigned roommate and discovered several references to bombing the school and taking mass casualties. When subsequently confronted, the student of concern explained that these simply reflected his creative side and sense of humor.

- A cheerleader advisor at a large university received an anonymous letter containing threats to disrupt collegiate sporting events and kill innocent people, including school children, unless authorities met seemingly bizarre demands, the nature of which pertained to network television coverage and the perceived discrimination against cheerleader squads outfitted in sleeveless tops.

- A human resources specialist reported the potentially problematic termination of a disgruntled employee who allegedly made multiple references to recent acts of school violence and commented on how easily such an incident could occur within the individual's own campus. The employee also reportedly threatened, "They better not fire me if they don't want the same thing here."

AN EFFECTIVE APPROACH

As a policing plan, a collaborative and standardized threat assessment protocol can prove valuable in addressing the various internal and external threats to campuses. Ideally, it involves flexible strategies to evaluate the range of observable behavioral factors (e.g., identified versus anonymous subject, the individual's motivations).

Threat assessment methodology considers contextual, target- and subject-specific, and behavioral factors to determine the risk of violence.[2] Different from profile-based techniques focused primarily on subject characteristics, models of this approach deal more with the interaction of the perpetrator's behavior, the target's vulnerability, and related factors.[3] Further, threat assessment differs from various surveys that evaluate site or asset vulnerabilities.[4]

A prevention-oriented strategy, threat assessment strives to accurately identify risks and to implement appropriate measures designed to minimize the potential for violence. To this end, investigators must evaluate the nature of the concerning (e.g., threatening or agitated) behaviors; the possible motives and nature of the displayed grievance; and the target's, or victim's, reaction. The nature and intensity of the threat posed depends on how far the subject has escalated along a chain of behaviors that move from ideation to threatened or problematic action.

LESSONS LEARNED
The experiences of law enforcement officers, as well as campus public safety personnel, administrators, and mental health practitioners, can provide valuable insight. The authors offer lessons learned from their own practice and from threat assessment literature.

AVOID TUNNEL VISION
When planning strategies to prevent and manage threats, authorities must recognize that campuses face them from a variety of sources, both internal and external, as indicated by the incidents addressed by BAU-1. While much attention focuses on violent students, public safety officials should resist a myopic approach and remain vigilant to all potential threats, recognizing that outsiders, employees, and other consumers of campus services may pose a threat to safety. Through comprehensive planning and collaboration, officials should anticipate multiple potential sources of violence and plan for copycat and hoax activity in the wake of highly publicized attacks at other institutions. While extreme acts of campus violence are rare, all stakeholders must consider themselves fortunate but not immune from the myriad safety concerns that plague colleges and universities across the nation.

RECOGNIZE CAMPUS VALUES
Safety policies must respect institutions as unique environments of higher learning. Acts of extreme violence often reflect hatred, intolerance, and bigotry, and people recognize that such behavior cannot be

tolerated within campus environments. Scholarship, creativity, and the fruitful exchange of ideas and learning could not thrive. Yet, the actual work of fusing pragmatic security measures with cherished Promethean ideals can prove challenging. Through education and outreach, campuses can allow safety planning and preparation to flourish as friends of an open campus environment.

In recognition of this balance, safety strategies should be flexible. Rigid policies (e.g., zero tolerance) do not necessarily promote secure environments and may contribute to outlandish applications of discipline that enrage and alienate the general campus populous. Administrators should review harsh disciplinary measures that may discourage individuals from reporting concerns and suspicions for fear a coworker or fellow student will face unjust punishment.

Communication must flow freely between consumers and providers. Students, faculty, and employees first must fully understand the mission of public safety before they can cooperate with and support it. Therefore, administrators and campus law enforcement personnel should seek opportunities to provide campus consumers with information concerning threat assessment reporting protocols, as well as information concerning confidentiality. Authorities should consider facilitating confidential reporting opportunities via text messaging, e-mail, and other web-based resources.

Attackers typically do not make direct threats to the targets, but they often "leak" their intentions to a range of bystanders. Perpetrators with hostile aspirations often manifest concerning behaviors, including ominous and menacing verbal statements; violent-themed content posted on social networking sites; and written assignments saturated with hatred, despair, and rage. Maximizing and streamlining the opportunities for these bystanders to recognize and report troubling behaviors remains one of the essential challenges faced by campus safety professionals.

ASSESS THREATENING COMMUNICATIONS

Assessing threatening or intimidating communications does not stifle creativity but, rather, represents a key aspect of maintaining a safe campus. Sometimes, faculty members may encounter disturbing or violent text or imagery from students while reviewing course assignments or conducting other classroom activities. Several noteworthy examples exist of subjects telegraphing or rehearsing violent intentions through text and video media. Though not all graphic or violent imagery necessarily predicts an individual's actions, campus personnel should report such content for a discrete threat assessment.

At a minimum, a student could be pleading for help through such disturbing messages. Faculty members may feel hesitant to report them for fear of creating a chilling effect within the classroom or alienating the student. However, a discrete threat assessment might allow campus law enforcement personnel and other professionals to not only gauge risk but also work with the faculty to develop strategies to approach the student.

Officials should evaluate drawings, essays, or videos that depict extreme acts of hostility, aggression, homicide, or suicide within the totality of the circumstances. Examining such products as part of an overall tapestry or mosaic further demonstrates the important role of the threat assessment team (TAT), which also can consider other pertinent factors, such as whether the student has actively sought to obtain items depicted in drawings (e.g., trench coats, weapons, masks).[5]

For instance, a student discloses to a mental health provider a particular resentment toward an individual. The counselor then learns that the subject has posted a video online in which he insults and disparages the person. A different video features the student shooting a handgun at a firing range. In a class assignment, the same subject writes of his overwhelming sense of despair and rage against the wealthy students at the university. Taken alone, each of these factors may not seem particularly dramatic, but, taken together, the TAT can begin to fully comprehend the true level of potential risk posed by the individual and manage it effectively.

SHARE RESPONSIBILITY

Recognizing the need to gather information on any particular subject from a variety of perspectives, threat management within the campus requires participation from multiple stakeholders, including, among others, student affairs, faculty, administrators, mental health care providers, and law enforcement officers—possibly municipal, considering the blended boundaries that often exist between on- and off-campus facilities. No single agency or other entity can manage the range of threats posed to university and college settings.

TATs should contemplate a holistic assessment and management strategy that considers the many aspects of the student's life—academic, residential, work, and social. Various colleges and universities have recognized the complexity of campus life and created teams designed to deal with crisis situations on campus, complemented by separate TATs designed to address long-term follow-up issues, such as treatment compliance and reintegration.

A TAT with diverse representation often will operate more efficiently and effectively. In one case, the BAU-1 evaluated a university student who, in the months following the shootings at Virginia Tech, had engaged in increasingly bizarre behaviors, to include the torturing of animals. The subject had collected photographs of friends and drawn target circles around the head and face of one individual. The student made numerous disturbing statements that included claiming he was the best shot in the state and asserting that he would be "the next Virginia Tech." Perhaps most disturbing, he had constructed a makeshift shooting range in his backyard for target practice.

The college's TAT had worked diligently in the months preceding this incident to establish lines of communication with external law enforcement agencies. Accordingly, the TAT activated an external network of allied agencies to identify crisis management strategies for reducing the potential for violence. Mental health practitioners and law enforcement officers and agents representing university, local, and federal organizations instantly collaborated to design and implement an intervention strategy.

Campus and municipal law enforcement officials located and interviewed the subject, then discovered that he had procured a semiautomatic handgun and a rifle. The student agreed to be voluntarily committed to a hospital for a mental health evaluation. Although he later revoked his permission, doctors had witnessed such disturbing behavior during their time with him that full commitment was authorized. One doctor considered the subject a "time bomb" who undoubtedly would have perpetrated an act of violence had the TAT not intervened. While this student was clearly engaged in disturbing behavior, the decision to intervene was enabled by preexisting channels of communication that facilitated a rapid and effective response.

Pinpoint Dangerous Individuals

Authorities should focus time and effort on individuals who actually pose a threat. Consistent across several studies and a central tenet of threat assessment literature—although some perpetrators may alert third parties or, perhaps, even their target—threatened violence does not necessarily predict that an individual ultimately will engage in the act.[6]

In the authors' experience, a direct but generic communicated threat to commit campus violence on a certain date (e.g., "I'm going to kill everyone in this library on May 9!") rarely materializes. By alerting public safety officials of their intent and the date of the attack, a threatener sets off a predictable chain of events resulting in additional security measures (e.g., bomb dogs, check points, evacuations) that ultimately reduces the chance for success.

Therefore, a communicated threat announcing the plan generally proves counterproductive to the plan itself. Of course, authorities must take all threats seriously and investigate them to the fullest feasible extent. However, campus safety professionals should remain aware of the clear distinction between threateners and attackers.

Do Not Rely on Expulsion

Except as a last resort and unless absolutely necessary to ensure campus safety, authorities should avoid the temptation to simply expel students of concern to quickly resolve a risk. Isolated from other contingency and safety planning, this strategy sometimes can worsen matters. The final humiliation of expulsion may serve as a precipitating, or triggering, stressor in the subject's life and propel the marginalized and hostile individual toward violence. Even after they physically remove the subject from the campus, officials will find it difficult, if not impossible, to prevent a determined student from returning. While expulsion remains an option, authorities must carefully consider the ramifications and limitations of such an action.

Students requiring discipline often can receive monitoring through mental health or other resources mandated by campus student services or judicial affairs offices more easily if not thrust unwillingly into the unstructured outside environment. Short of subjects displaying some extremely troubling behaviors that warrant immediate expulsion, campus professionals and law enforcement officers may collaborate to monitor such individuals on a probationary status. Officials should consider the potential for such monitoring on a case-by-case basis.

Rather than isolating the subject and possibly exacerbating existing grievances, university officials can explore ways to integrate the student into an environment where monitoring and treatment coexist with safety and security. For instance, authorities can make appropriate referrals, with follow-up, to social services, mental health, and psychological counseling resources.

Although officials must ensure the overall safety of the campus, they can benefit from a supervised integration, rather than isolation, of the individual. Doing so allows them to put the student into a supportive educational environment and to monitor, reinforce, and adjust interventional treatment strategies.

Also, in certain cases involving a student separated from the university, authorities should consider reintegrating the individual, provided the maintenance of appropriate safeguards. Presumably, students who suffer from a serious physical or medical condition will have the approval to pause studies, receive treatment, and return to classes with full privileges. While these individuals clearly present an entirely different scenario from those who pose a threat, it may be worthwhile to consider reintegrating a student who receives appropriate mental health care, treatment, and counseling and who demonstrates a record of compliance with security and treatment parameters.

If a subject presents safety concerns far too serious for reintegration to the campus environment, officials should consider active engagement in a process to ensure that the individual is not left adrift and isolated. While campus authorities do not traditionally take responsibility for assisting in students' lives once they leave the institution, it seems prudent to adopt a long-term threat-management perspective, collaborate with outside agencies, and become an active participant in the process to minimize the potential risk an individual still could pose to the campus. Campus safety professionals should check with legal counsel to verify that such contact with and monitoring of a former student is permitted.

Officials may find that some students are suitable candidates for nontraditional or creative arrangements that enhance security without exacerbating or increasing the risk of violence. For example, a community college received reports of disturbing behavior from a male student making troubling statements and stalking females. Although only one semester from graduating, his behavior had escalated to the point that he could not remain on campus. Expelling this student potentially could have stoked resentment while simultaneously cutting off the college's ability to monitor his moods, statements, and behaviors.

Thinking creatively, officials arranged for him to receive video-recorded copies of classes at his off-campus residence. An administrator who previously had positive interactions with the student and who had the individual's trust served as a primary point of contact. The administrator maintained regular interaction with the student to ensure the completion of his assignments and, more important, to gauge his level of anger and his disposition. The individual successfully completed assignments via e-mail, graduated on time, and avoided becoming further disenfranchised as a result of an expulsion.

USE A SINGLE POINT OF CONTACT
When monitoring cases, campus safety professionals should consider providing a single contact (i.e., a "temperature taker") to a subject. The initial intervention with a student may prove insufficient as additional follow-up may be necessary. In some cases, continued monitoring of the subject's behavior or communications will be needed. Either way, someone must have responsibility for monitoring or conducting follow-up of the situation. Given that multiple campus entities could partner to provide support, authorities must ensure communications to a subject are consistent and "on the same page" to avoid confusion.

A CAMPUS EXAMPLE
Campus authorities can perform collaborative threat assessment and management activities by organizing existing resources. It is critical to have one entity responsible for coordinating and monitoring situations. The University of Nebraska-Lincoln (UNL) has successfully implemented a TAT that has addressed dozens of situations. It consists of officers specially trained in threat assessment, as well as a consulting psychologist. Other campus personnel (such as those in human resources and mental health and student services) participate on an as-needed basis. The university's police department has primary responsibility for the security of the campus and

properties and the investigation of criminal incidents occurring on university grounds.

University stakeholders can make a referral for a threat assessment when encountering a concerning behavior, and, through various campus educational activities, the TAT encourages them to do so. In addition to training sessions to encourage prevention and early reporting, TAT members also reach out to human resources and student affairs staff with guidelines and criteria for use in screening for problematic student or employee issues that may raise concerns or warrant referrals.

The TAT also monitors campus and local police contacts for incidents (e.g., domestic violence, protection orders, stalking allegations) that may warrant further assessment or monitoring of potential threats to the campus setting. Additionally, TAT members coordinate interventions with other university services, as well as monitor situations as warranted, to ensure that there is no flare-up of a posed threat. As a key focus, the TAT has educated and collaborated with a wide range of university stakeholder groups.

CONCLUSION
Colleges and universities strive to attain the noble goal of making society better. Unfortunately, recent events have highlighted the reality that not even these institutions of higher learning are immune to unthinkable acts.

Of course, campus and law enforcement authorities want to address this problem and keep students, faculty, and others safe. While all segments of society, including campuses, face danger of some sort, by incorporating effective threat assessment and management strategies, officials can put measures in place that will meet this challenge head-on.

ENDNOTES

1 Throughout this article, the authors refer to campus law enforcement in general terms. They understand that campuses may vary regarding the presence and amount of law enforcement and public safety officers.

2 J. Berglund, R. Borum, R. Fein, and B. Vossekuil, "Threat Assessment: Defining an approach for Evaluating Risk of Targeted Violence," *Behavioral Sciences and the Law* 17 (1999): 323-337; and M.J. Scalora, D.G. Wells, and W. Zimmerman, "Use of Threat Assessment for the Protection of Congress," in *Stalking, Threats, and Attacks Against Public Figures*, ed. J. Hoffman, J.R. Meloy, and L. Sheridan (New York, NY: Oxford University Press, 2008).

3 J. Berglund, R. Borum, R. Fein, W. Modzeleski, M. Reddy, and B. Vossekuil, "Evaluating Risk for Targeted Violence in Schools: Comparing Risk Assessment, Threat Assessment, and Other Approaches," *Psychology in the Schools* 38 (2001): 157-172.

4 U.S. Department of Justice, National Institute of Justice, *Threat Assessment: An Approach to Prevent Targeted Violence* (Washington, D.C., 1995).

5 A standard definition of TATs does not exist. Generally, such teams are multidisciplinary in nature, bringing together campus professionals responsible for safety and behavioral management (e.g., campus safety, law enforcement, mental health, EAP, human resources, and student affairs personnel). Team composition also may vary based upon the focus of the TAT (e.g., issues pertaining to students or personnel, external threats), as well as the resources available given the size of the institution.

6 *Threat Assessment: An Approach to Prevent Targeted Violence.*

DISCUSSION QUESTIONS

1. Who do you think should serve on a campus threat assessment team, and what should their roles be?

2. What do you think is meant by the term "threat"? What must be said or done in order for there to be a threat that warrants further inquiry?

CRITICAL THINKING EXERCISE

I worked a threat assessment in the past where a college student who lived in a dormitory posted images of himself on a social media network with firearms in each hand, and taking a pose similar to that of the Virginia Tech shooter Seung-Hui Cho. His posting indicated what university he attended, and a third-party, after viewing the images, notified the university.

Against my advice, campus officials sent a lone student services representative to speak to the student and assess the situation. The staff member subsequently stated that he did not believe the student had any weapons in his dorm room and did not pose a threat to the community. The reason the police did not go to the student's room in the first instance was based upon advice that their presence might "escalate" the situation. After consulting with threat assessment colleagues, I insisted that the police go to the dormitory and seek consent to search, which they did. There they found loaded semiautomatic pistols, shotguns, rifles, knives, and an abundance of ammunition, all of which were seized.

Discuss how this situation may have been better handled from the outset up until the point of the weapons seizure. The second part of the assignment is to discuss the proper steps from the point of the weapons seizure.

Addressing School Violence

By

Brandi Booth, Ph.D.; Vincent B. Van Hasselt, Ph.D.;
and Gregory M. Vecchi, Ph.D.

May 2011: FBI Law Enforcement Bulletin

INCIDENTS, SUCH AS THE RECENT ONES AT COLUMBINE, Virginia Tech, and Northern Illinois University, produce horrifying, enduring images. Members of the mass media publicize and inadvertently glorify these events to capture the attention of viewers and readers. Unfortunately, many of the portrayals have led to faulty assumptions and stereotypes of the school violence perpetrator. Further, researchers have devoted much attention to generating a working profile of these offenders and describing many typical characteristics.

However, it is important to caution against the use of a profile because many apparent warning signs may be irrelevant and restrictive and even could unfairly categorize a student who may not pose danger.[1] Therefore, an awareness of the potential warning signs empirically based in making accurate threat assessments in the school setting proves critical.

CURRENT STATISTICS

Homicides in schools have decreased since 1994 despite periods of copycat shootings during the late 1990s and 2007 to 2008.[2] However, simple and aggravated assaults, as well as drug/narcotic and weapon

violations, increased between 2000 and 2004.[3] Bullying remains one of the largest problems in schools, with the percentage of students reportedly bullied at least once per week steadily increasing since 1999.[4] According to the FBI's Uniform Crime Reporting Program, school offenders typically are Caucasian males between the ages of 13 and 18. However, the number of girls involved in school crime has increased from over 12,000 incidents in 2000 to approximately 25,000 occurrences in 2005.[5] This included crimes ranging from those against property and society (e.g., criminal mischief, burglary, and drug/narcotic violations) to offenses against persons (e.g., assault, manslaughter, and murder).

WARNING SIGNS

Many factors can contribute to the development of a violent school offender. These include family, school, and social dynamics, as well as the [personality characteristics] of the child.[6]

FAMILY DYNAMICS

Family dynamics include the thinking, traditions, beliefs, and behavior patterns within the home. These play a vital role in the social development of a young child. It is important to question how these dynamics affect and are perceived by the student.[7] For example, an abusive marriage or a particularly hostile divorce can have damaging effects on children. An adolescent who lives in a chaotic and neglectful home environment may develop poor coping and social skills and behavior problems primarily due to exposure to violence and inadequate parenting.[8] Not surprisingly, research has shown that in terms of the child's long-term social and emotional development, having one nurturing, attentive, and caring parent is better than two in a relationship characterized by discord or abuse.[9]

Although negative family dynamics play a role in the development of violent tendencies, many high-profile cases of school violence seem to have involved children from a positive home environment. For instance, Kip Kinkel, an individual who murdered both of his parents before killing two students and wounding 25 others in Oregon, appeared to come from an ideal family (two parents, upper-middleclass home, successful older sibling). However, a closer examination revealed a highly critical father and a child who perceived himself as inadequate, was physically awkward, and had a fascination with guns and bombs. In fact, to support Kip's interest, his father bought him firearms.

Several of the larger, more publicized school shootings took place in middle-class neighborhoods. People have raised many questions as to why these homicides occur in such areas. Experts have suggested that overly permissive or uninvolved parents of these children bear some responsibility.[10]

SCHOOL DYNAMICS
School dynamics are the customs, beliefs, and patterns of behavior that comprise the campus culture.[11] A student's role in these dynamics offers insight into the individual's behavior and self-perception. Knowing a school's dynamics sheds light on what students value, which adolescents more likely will gain approval or be bullied, and which receive attention from authorities.[12]

Bullying is a major factor and has a strong impact on a child or adolescent. In a study of 15 school shootings between 1995 and 2001, rejection (e.g., bullying, ostracism, and romantic rejection) contributed to the violent behavior.[13] Peer victimization and poor quality of interpersonal and romantic relationships can contribute to student depression.[14] Once these individuals feel rejected, they may begin to identify with others who feel socially shunned or who belong to a deviant peer group. This may contribute to the proliferation and acceptance of violence.[15]

FOUR MAIN AREAS OF EXAMINATION

1. Family Dynamics: Family's thinking, traditions, beliefs, and patterns of behavior
2. School Dynamics: Schools's customs, beliefs, and behavioral patterns (e.g., bullying, treatment of students, some individuals receiving more/less attention, school activities)
3. Social Dynamics: Student's beliefs and attitudes toward drugs, friends, weapons, entertainment, and other activities (e.g., violent video games)
4. Characteristics/Personality: Leakage, depression, verbal expressions, bizarre actions, thoughts/obsessions, and physical behaviors

Cyber bullying also is on the rise, with students engaging in verbally aggressive behavior on social networking sites, such as MySpace and Facebook, and instant-messenger services.[16] Adolescents are extremely sensitive to rejection and the opinions of peers, both of which can serve as catalysts for revenge. Any bullying should be seriously assessed as it can be indicative of more serious problems, such as fighting and weapon carrying.[17]

- Leakage: boasts, predictions, and subtle threats; stories, essays, poems, and pictures; violent fantasies; and interest in violent video games, movies, and books

- Depression, anger, impulsive and uncontrollable behavior
- Poor coping skills
- Low frustration tolerance
- Grudges, lack of resiliency
- "Us against them" mentality, narcissism
- Boastfulness about weapons, abusive language
- Suicidal ideation, wishes of death, desire to kill others
- Delusions, hallucinations, bizarre thoughts
- History of physical assault
- Perpetrator or victim of bullying
- Substance abuse
- Rebellion against authority
- Isolated, withdrawn
- Fatigue

SOCIAL DYNAMICS

Social dynamics of the community provide information on a child's preferred lifestyle. They also influence attitudes and beliefs toward drugs, friends, weapons, and entertainment.[18] The diaries of the Columbine shooters, Dylan Klebold and Eric Harris, suggest addictive behavior with first-person-shooter video games.[19]

Although the level of their influence is controversial, violent video games can have a detrimental impact on vulnerable adolescents and even college-age students. For example, one study found that girls often will become more verbally aggressive after exposure to violent video games.[20] While this does not mean that playing such games leads to homicidal acts, doing so can serve as a facilitator for impressionable adolescents who may not see any other outlet for their psychological pain.

PERSONALITY CHARACTERISTICS

The personality of the student proves critical in assessing the potential for violence. Certain traits of a child or adolescent raise concern. In particular, individuals who eventually commit school homicides exhibit behavior "leakage."[21] This refers to a student's intentional or unintentional disclosure of thoughts, fantasies, feelings, and possible intentions. Examples include boasts, predictions, subtle threats, stories, essays, poems, and drawings. Leakage also can take the form of a fascination with violence and violent entertainment (e.g., video games and movies). It appears that nearly 50 percent of school homicide perpetrators exhibit some type of warning sign, including leaving notes or making a verbal threat.[22]

A student also may show signs of depression, often manifested in adolescents by anger and irritability. Additionally, the individual could display low frustration tolerance, poor coping skills, and a lack of resiliency when faced with stressful situations or conflicts (e.g., end of a romantic relationship). This becomes compounded by bullying at school or hostility at home. Consequently, the student may blame others, demonstrate a lack of empathy, and exhibit an exaggerated sense of entitlement. An "us against them" mentality reflects the latter. The individual even may criticize previous school shooters for their failures (e.g., not getting a high enough body count).[23]

INTRAPERSONAL VARIABLES

An examination of intrapersonal variables includes verbal communication, thoughts, and behaviors.[24] These tend to be more salient, easier to observe, and often deemed leakage prior to more offensive and violent behavior.

VERBAL COMMUNICATION

Verbal warning signs include a student's oral and

written communication.[25] A common misconception holds that violent people just "snap." In fact, in over 75 percent of school shooting incidents, students knew beforehand about the troubled adolescent and the planned event.[26] This is because the shooter may make direct threats, brag about bringing weapons to school, use abusive language, or verbalize a wish to kill others and even to be killed.

COGNITIONS

The student may exhibit bizarre thoughts, such as delusions, hallucinations, paranoia, or other disrupted mental processes. Further, the individual may write with profanity and abusive language, which tends to be extreme and contextually inappropriate; this suggests a deteriorating mental capacity and a deficiency of emotional control.

Eric Harris and Seung-Hui Cho, the Virginia Tech perpetrator, serve as good examples of this behavior. Their disjointed and violent rants were both written and oral. Such bizarre thoughts (as determined by individuals' verbalizations), may indicate a serious mental health condition, especially because schizophrenia and other major psychiatric disorders have their initial onset in the late teens and early 20s. Thoughts of suicide or dying in the process of their planned actions often accompany violent adolescents.

BEHAVIORS

Behavioral and physical warning signs indicative of a violent student include a prior history of physical assault, being both a bully and a victim of bullying, and possession of weapons and violent literature. The individual also may have a history of substance use, rebelliousness against authority, and socially isolated and withdrawn behavior.[27] The latter may point to depression, often manifested as irritability and anger in children and youths.

Effective Measures

Threat Assessment

Threat assessment in the campus setting involves law enforcement and school officials working collaboratively to determine risk.[28] It consists of evaluating a threat, reaching a conclusion regarding threat level, and determining an effective response.[29] This approach, developed by the U.S. Secret Service, is based on six key principles.

- Violence is not unpredictable or spontaneous; therefore, information about the student, as well as the pupil's behavior, can prevent violence.

- Information should include knowledge about the student, environment, specific situation, and target of the violence.

- All information should be verifiable and reliable.

- Authorities should leave out assumptions or subjective impressions about the student's personality or other characteristics and instead base evaluations on facts and observable behaviors. The warning signs should be used more as guidelines than absolutes.

- Multiple sources of information (e.g., other students, teachers, faculty, and parents) should be obtained.

- Conclusions should support the facts as to whether the student poses a threat, not necessarily whether the individual made a threat. Also, assessments should include considerations of whether the subject has the means and intent to carry it out.[30]

PREVENTION PROGRAMS

School resource officer (SRO) programs serve an integral role in threat assessment. [31] In times of crisis, having an SRO based in the school decreases response time and increases student and staff perceptions of safety.[32] The SRO also can educate students about the consequences of their behavior and identify peer conflicts.[33] The value of SROs further can be enhanced by their heightened awareness of warning signs and cues relevant in accurate threat assessment.

Over the past several years, police agencies have established a positive working relationship with school districts and students through SRO and Drug Abuse Resistance Education (DARE) programs. Law enforcement officers can contribute to violence prevention in several ways.

First, they must have an ongoing collaboration with teachers and administrators. Second, they must be capable of conducting their own assessments of bullying and related problems in their schools. Third, law enforcement personnel in schools should become well acquainted with students and staff and make themselves accessible for reporting of information; an anonymous reporting system is advisable to encourage students to come forward with important tips.[34]

The National School Safety Center has offered suggestions for decreasing campus violence and strengthening the relationship between law enforcement and school districts. For example, an understanding and written agreement should exist about how the school and police agency will work together to promote violence prevention and respond to crises. An Officer Friendly program can be established whereby SROs provide instruction on a variety of topics, such as drug abuse, juvenile justice, and child safety. Students can be encouraged to go on ride-alongs with officers, and a Big Brother/Big Sister program also can be implemented, pairing students with law enforcement personnel. The Police Athletic League historically has had success in forging such relationships as well. These strategies will increase the cohesiveness between police officers and students and facilitate communication and information flow between the two.[36] The International Association of Campus Law Enforcement Administrators and the National Association of School Safety and Law Enforcement Officers provide information on how officers should become involved and respond to threats and crises and collaborate with local school districts.

SCHOOL SAFETY PLAN

Each school should have a safety plan. Law enforcement must have an active role in the plan's development and implementation. The plan should outline prevention programs, including the SRO's role within the school community, and bullying prevention programs. Further, it should indicate that a threat assessment team (TAT) will form and activate upon determination of a threat. If the threat has been assessed as real and imminent, steps in formulating a response must be outlined. Each school must have an established policy of contingency management that includes detention, suspension, and expulsion. Authorities should make parents aware of initiatives to prevent violence and the intervention plan upon identifying a threat.

Officials also must notify parents when someone has been threatened, keeping in mind privacy and defamation- of-character laws.[37] Also, search-and-seizure laws must be considered when assessing a threat. Authorities should conduct interviews with the individual who made the threat, as well as any witnesses and potential targets. The TAT should convene to discuss the results of the interview, determine whether a threat is imminent and formulate a response plan if necessary.[38] Mental health officials should be consulted in cases when hospitalization due to a possible psychiatric disorder (e.g., depression, suicide, psychosis) is required.[39]

CASE EXAMPLE

The case of Kip Kinkel demonstrates a family life that appeared pleasant and nurturing.[35] However, other warning signs indicate a bullied and troubled child who had difficulties in academics, feelings of alienation, arrest and psychiatric histories, and suicidal tendencies.

Kip Kinkel was born in 1982. His parents both taught Spanish, his father at a community college and his mother at a local high school. Kip's older sister by approximately six years excelled in both academics and athletics.

His family moved to Spain for one year when Kip was six years old. He attended a non-English speaking school and had difficulty adapting; however, his sister performed well. During his schooling in Spain, Kip frequently faced bullying and felt alienated. When the family returned to the United States, Kip's teachers noticed that he was developmentally immature and behind in school. As a result, he repeated first grade. In fourth grade, he was diagnosed with dyslexia.

Kip showed an interest in explosives and firearms in the seventh grade, when he purchased books on how to build a bomb. In eighth grade, he was arrested for shoplifting and suspended for kicking another student. As a result, he was referred for a psychological evaluation, diagnosed with depression, and placed on antidepressant medication. During his court-ordered psychiatric treatment, authorities considered Kip to have early onset schizophrenia, but he initially denied any thought disorder (e.g., hallucinations, delusions). In fact, months before the shooting, his sister reported a pleasant family vacation. However, in 1998, he exploded in an English class, screaming, "Damn these voices in my head." He stated that in sixth grade he began hearing them tell him that he was not worth anything.

Kip also was noted to have strange delusions, including ideas that the Chinese planned to invade America, Disney would take over the world, and that microchips were planted in his head. He also made several morbid and cryptic drawings, including one that stated, "Killers start sad and crazy."

He received psychiatric treatment until approximately July 1997 and maintained his antidepressant regimen. During that time, without his parents knowledge, he bought his first sawedoff shotgun from a friend. However, his father bought him a 9-millimeter Glock and, later, a .22-caliber semiautomatic rifle.

It is speculated that his parents were concerned about his interest, but wanted to educate him about gun safety. In an interview, Kip's sister indicated that his parents had tried everything to help him. He expressed to his family his interest in how bombs and guns work, as well as his desire to enter law enforcement after college. In fact, Kip's sister noted that violence did not occur in the family; rather, she perceived a positive family environment. However, Kip's feelings of inadequacy were apparent.

Later that fall, Kip's psychiatrist discontinued his antidepressant medication. During this time, Kip made a speech in class about how to make a bomb. Throughout the school year of 1997 to 1998, several school shootings occurred in the nation, including those in Pearl, Mississippi; West Paducah, Kentucky; and Jonesboro, Arkansas. In May 1998, Kip, at age 15, arranged to buy a .32-caliber pistol from a friend. When the friend's father reported it missing, Kip was expelled for bringing it to school. His father picked him up from the police station; reports indicated that Kip was upset for disappointing his parents. In her interview, his sister stated that disappointing their parents was the biggest offense in the family.

That afternoon and early evening, Kip killed both of his parents. The next day, he dressed in a trench coat, carried three guns, and taped a hunting knife to his leg. He shot 27 students; 2 died, and 25 were injured. Some students tackled him and held him down until police arrived. Once in police custody, he charged an officer with the knife and shouted that he wanted to be killed. In his confession, Kip exclaimed that he was hearing voices and once again shouted, "Damn these voices in my head."

CONCLUSION
Despite the decline in the rates of homicides committed by adolescents over the past decade, the potential for violent behavior among students remains. However, school and law enforcement officials can work together to reduce the threat of such violence.

Understanding the warning signs—including family, school, and social dynamics, as well as personality characteristics— proves important for threat assessment. An analysis of a student's verbal communications, cognitions, and overt behaviors should be part of the threat assessment strategy. A positive and collaborative relationship between law enforcement personnel and students can increase information flow and enhance the accuracy and effectiveness of threat assessments. Also essential are close working relationships between law enforcement personnel and school administrators, teachers, and parents.

ENDNOTES

[1] M.E. O'Toole, U.S. Department of Justice, Federal Bureau of Investigation, National Center for the Analysis of Violent Crime, *The School Shooter: A Threat Assessment Perspective* (Quantico, VA, 1999).

[2] U.S. Department of Education, National Center for Education Statistics, *Indicators of School Crime and Safety*, (Washington, DC, 2007).

[3] J.H. Noonan and M.C. Vavra, U.S. Department of Justice, Federal Bureau of Investigation, Criminal Justice Information Services Division, *Crime in Schools and Colleges: A Study of Offenders and Arrestees Reported via National Incident- Based Reporting System Data* (Clarksburg, WV, 2007).

[4] *Indicators of School Crime and Safety.*

[5] Noonan and Vavra.

[6] O'Toole.

[7] O'Toole.

[8] L.A. McCloskey, A.J. Figueredo, and M.P. Koss, "The Effects of Systemic Family Violence on Children's Mental Health," *Child Development* 66, no. 5 (1995): 1239-1261; and J. Osofsky, "The Impact of Violence on Children," *The Future of Children* 9, no. 3 (1999): 33-49.

[9] C. Casanueva, S.L. Martin, D.K. Runyan, R.P. Barth, and R.H. Bradley, "Quality of Maternal Parenting Among Intimate- Partner Violence Victims Involved with the Child Welfare System," *Journal of Family Violence* 23 (2008): 413-427.

[10] S.W. Twemlow, "Assessing Adolescents Who Threaten Homicide in Schools: A Recent Update," *Clinical Social Work Journal* 36 (2008): 127-129.

[11] O'Toole.

[12] O'Toole.

[13] M.R. Leary, R.M. Kowalski, L. Smith, and S. Phillips, "Teasing, Rejection, and Violence: Case Studies of the School Shootings," *Aggressive Behavior* 29, no. 3 (2003): 202-214.

[14] A.M. LaGreca and H.M. Harrison, "Adolescent Peer Relationships, Friendships, and Romantic Relationships: Do They Predict Social Anxiety and Depression?" *Journal of Clinical Child and Adolescent Psychology* 34, no. 1 (2005): 49-61.

[15] S. Verlinden, M. Hersen, and J. Thomas, "Risk Factors in School Shootings," *Clinical Psychology Review* 20 (2000): 3-56.

[16] A. Harmon, "Internet Gives Teenage Bullies Weapons to Wound from Afar," *New York Times*, August 26, 2004.

[17] T.R. Nansel, M.D. Overpeck, D.L. Haynie, W.J. Ruan, and P.C. Scheidt, "Relationships Between Bullying and
Violence Among U.S. Youth," *Archives of Pediatrics and Adolescent Medicine* 157, no. 4 (2003): 248-353.

[18] O'Toole.

[19] Casanueva, Martin, Runyan, Barth, and Bradley.

[20] C.A. Anderson and K.E. Dill, "Video Games and Aggressive Thoughts, Feelings, and Behavior in the Laboratory and in Life, "*Journal of Personality and Social Psychology* 78, no. 4 (2000): 772-790.

[21] K. Mohandie, School Violence Threat Assessment (San Diego, CA: Specialized Training Services, 2000); and O'Toole.

[22] American Medical Association, "School-Associated Violent Deaths in the United States, 1994-
1999," *Journal of the American Medical Association* 286, no. 21 (2001): 2695-2702.

[23] O'Toole.

[24] G.M. Vecchi, "CONFLICT AND CRISIS COMMUNICATION—Workplace and School Violence, Stockholm Syndrome, and Abnormal Psychology," *Annals of American Psychotherapy* 12, no. 3 (2009): 30-39; and J.A. Daniels, T.E. Royster, and G.M. Vecchi, "Barricaded Hostage and Crisis Situations in Schools: A Review of Recent Incidents," in *Proceedings of Persistently Safe Schools: The 2007 National Conference on Safe Schools*, ed. D.L. White,

B.C. Glenn, and A. Wimes (Washington, DC: Hamilton Fish Institute, The George Washington University, 2007), 61-67.

[25] Harmon.

[26] Harmon.

[27] Harmon.

[28] O'Toole.

[29] O'Toole.

[30] For more information about SRO programs and training, visit the National Association of School Resource Officers Web site at *http://www.nasro.org.*

[31] O'Toole; and P. Finn, "School Resource Officer Programs," FBI Law Enforcement Bulletin, August 2006,
1-7.

[32] O'Toole.

[33] U.S. Department of Health and Human Services, "Involvement of Law Enforcement Officers in Bullying Prevention," (accessed May 20, 2010).

[34] National School Safety Center Web site, *http//:www.nssc1.org* (accessed May 20, 2010).

[35] PBS Frontline, "Frontline: The Killer at Thurston High," *http://www.pbs.org/wgbh/pages/frontline/shows/kinkel/* (accessed May 20, 2010).

[36] Nansel, Overpeck, Haynie, Ruan, and Scheidt.

[37] Nansel, Overpeck, Haynie, Ruan, and Scheidt.

[38] Nansel, Overpeck, Haynie, Ruan, and Scheidt.

[39] Nansel, Overpeck, Haynie, Ruan, and Scheidt.

DISCUSSION QUESTIONS

1. Drawing from information contained in this article, what proactive steps might be considered in minimizing school violence amongst students even before threats have been made?

2. Where do you think the line should be drawn (if at all) between the privacy of the students (academic, medical, and other records or issues), and the need to protect the community. Where is the proper balance?

CRITICAL THINKING EXERCISE

According to Meloy and colleagues (2014),* there are several typologies of warning behaviors, which can be grouped as follows:

1. Pathway

2. Fixation

3. Identification

4. Pseudo-Commando

5. Novel Aggression

6. Energy Burst

7. Leakage

8. Last Resort

9. Directly Communicated Threat

Your assignment is to research these typologies of warning behaviors. Next, based upon what is written in this article, attempt to match the typologies to facts in the article including actual events that are discussed therein.

*Meloy, J. R., Hoffman, J. Roshdi, K., Glaz-Ocik, J., & Gludimann, A. (2014). Warning behaviors and their configurations across various domains of targeted violence. In J. R. Meloy & J. Hoffmann (Eds.), *International handbook of threat assessment* (pp. 39-53). New York, NY: Oxford University Press.

ADDRESSING THE PROBLEM OF THE ACTIVE SHOOTER
By Katherine W. Schweit, J.D.

May 2013: *FBI Law Enforcement Bulletin*

UNFORTUNATELY, SCENES INVOLVING ACTIVE SHOOTERS have become too familiar. Radio transmissions of possible shots fired send the closest police officers to the scene. In today's world, such calls carry with them the memories of school, business, and theater shootings.

Responding officers must recognize that more than half of mass-shooting incidents—57 percent—still will be underway, with 75 percent requiring law enforcement personnel to confront the perpetrator before the threat ends.[1] And, one-third of those officers will be shot as they engage.[2]

CRITICAL NEED
That number disturbs FBI Section Chief (SC) Christopher Combs, Strategic Information and Operations Center, the FBI's central command post for all major incidents. He also leads a bureau team assigned by the White House to find ways to support state, local, tribal, and campus law enforcement officers who may face an active-shooter situation. The team's efforts comprise part of a larger initiative, Now Is the Time, begun by the White House after the mass

killing of young children at Sandy Hook Elementary School in Newtown, Connecticut.[3]

First responders face the threat of force as part of their daily jobs. Although tactical teams, such as SWAT, train for barricade situations and multiple-member entries, active-shooter training focuses on five-person-or-less building entries. Responding officers may not previously have trained to face this unique type of threat. According to SC Combs, "We've been asked to do our part to help law enforcement better prepare for the next Newtown. With so many officers engaged in shootings, it's important we do whatever we can to help try to change that and make them safer."

IMPORTANT TRAINING

The U.S. Department of Justice (DOJ), Bureau of Justice Assistance (BJA) partially has funded—through its VALOR initiative—the Advanced Law Enforcement Rapid Response Training (ALERRT) course, an active-shooter training program.[4] Born from concerns that arose from shootings at Columbine High School in Littleton, Colorado, ALERRT better prepares the first officers on the scene of an active-shooter situation. The training was developed by the San Marcos, Texas, Police Department and the Hays County, Texas, Sheriff's Department and adopted by Texas State University, San Marcos.

In the aftermath of the tragedy in Sandy Hook, Connecticut, the FBI offered to partner with BJA in the delivery of this crucial training and sent its tactical instructors (TIs) to attend and assess the ALERRT course. The TI program is managed by the Training Division at Quantico, Virginia. As word of training has spread, news of the learning opportunities went national. Since its inception in 2002, ALERRT has trained more than 40,000 law enforcement officers as a result of more than $26 million in funding.

The 16-hour Basic Active-Shooter Course, one of several courses offered, prepares first responders to isolate, distract, and end the threat when an active shooter is engaged. The course covers shooting and moving, conducting threshold evaluations, employing concepts and principles of team movement, using setup and room entry techniques, approaching and breaching the crisis site, practicing rescue-team tactics, handling improvised explosive devices, and recognizing postengagement priorities of work. Training teams carry training-ammunition kits, allowing up to 30 students to engage in tactical force-on-force scenarios carried out in unoccupied schools or office buildings.

Virtually every state has officers trained through the ALERRT program, and many have made the training mandatory for active-shooter responders, the first among them Mississippi, Alabama, Iowa, Louisiana, and South Carolina. Since the Sandy Hook tragedy, more police departments have requested training.

NATIONAL STANDARD, NATIONAL TRAINING
Aware of the increased demand, the FBI agreed to supplement BJA's effort and integrated ALERRT into the White House initiative, reasoning the training could provide added support for law enforcement officers most at risk—those first on the scene. A private study of 35 active-shooter incidents during 2012 found that 37 percent of the attacks ended in less than 5 minutes, 63 percent in less than 15 minutes.[5] Minutes into the Sikh temple shooting in Oak Creek, Wisconsin, the perpetrator turned away from other victims to engage the first officer on the scene and shot him 15 times. Fortunately, the officer survived.[6]

To assist in this project, SC Combs and his team turned to the Tactical Instructors (TIs) in the Law

Enforcement Training for Safety and Survival (LETSS) program, which was developed in 1992. LETSS, a program of the Practical Applications Unit in the FBI's Training Division, strives to provide officers with the skills and mind-set required to identify and handle critical situations in high-risk environments.[7]

LETSS experts recognized the need for coordinated and standardized nationwide active-shooter training and through the FBI/BJA partnership began working directly with ALERRT personnel to study how best to resolve these situations. TIs traveled to the ALERRT center in Texas to observe protocols and ask questions. After working with ALERRT personnel to adjust the course by providing updates and ensuring compliance with current rules and regulations, the FBI adopted the modified course as a national standard.

Since February, 100 FBI TIs have attended the 5-day ALERRT Train-the-Trainer school in San Marcos, Texas. The FBI recognizes that it best serves in a support role as a training partner with BJA. These certified TIs, along with ALERRT instructors, now jointly will be able to provide the 16-hour training at no cost to agencies across the nation. Although funding remains a challenge as federal budget cuts continue, a strong commitment exists to continue to support active-shooter training.

Statistics show that 98 percent of active-shooter incidents involve state and local crimes, primarily occurring in areas with small- and medium-sized law enforcement agencies.[8] Ninety-eight percent of these crimes are carried out by a single shooter, usually male (97 percent).[9]

IMPORTANT DIRECTIVE
On January 14, 2013, President Barack Obama signed the Investigative Assistance for Violent Crimes Act of

2012 into law. The act permits the attorney general, upon the request of an appropriate state or local law enforcement officer, to provide assistance in the investigation of 1) violent acts and shootings occurring in a "place of public use" and 2) mass killings—defined as three or more killings in a single incident—and attempted mass killings. Under the act, federal officials assisting the investigation of these incidents are presumed to be acting within the scope of their employment.

The FBI's efforts include three areas of support. First, before an incident occurs, agencies can obtain no-cost, active-shooter training close to home by submitting a request via the ALERRT website, *http://www.alerrt.org.* The site provides general information, requirements for hosting a school in a particular area, and registration materials. Department officials also can call the special agent in charge of their local FBI field office for further registration assistance.

Second, experts in the FBI's Behavioral Analysis Unit (BAU) are available to conduct threat assessments and develop threat mitigation strategies for persons of concern. BAU is part of the FBI's Critical Incident Response Group, home to the FBI's most sophisticated tactical assets. Each FBI field office has a BAU representative to the FBI's National Center for the Analysis of Violent Crimes (NCAVC). The NCAVC focuses its efforts not on how to respond tactically to an active-shooter situation, but, rather, how to prevent one. These experts can work as part of a team to prevent a situation from escalating by identifying, assessing, and managing the threat.

Third, all FBI field offices are hosting a series of two-day crisis management conferences during 2013 to engage with their state, local, tribal, and campus law enforcement partners and share lessons learned and best practices. The conferences afford attendees an opportunity to share and hear details gleaned from the many after-action reviews the FBI has participated in and observed with involved law enforcement agencies. These provide a plethora of details on how best to deal with unique and complex aspects of these situations, as well as FBI resources available to assist in incident response, management, and resolution.

Conference topics include pre-event and behavioral indicators, evidence collection, complex crime-scene management, strategies to deal with the national news media, procedures for handling IEDs, and methods of providing victim assistance to families and first responders.

Conferences are followed by a newly developed four-hour tabletop exercise for law enforcement agencies and other first responders based on facts relating to the recent school shootings. A second tabletop rolling out in May was specifically designed for college campus incidents. These are designed around the latest lessons learned and best management practices, which will include participation by law enforcement, first responders, fire departments, and other Emergency / public safety agencies.

CONCLUSION
Agencies interested in active-shooter training, conferences, tabletop exercises, or threat-analysis assistance should contact their local FBI office. Doing so may help counter the threat posed by the active shooter. These important educational opportunities may help save civilian lives, as well as the first responders who come to their aid.

ENDNOTES

[1] Author follow-on analysis of data from J. Pete Blair and M. Hunter Martaindale, "United States Active Shooter Events from 2000 to 2010: Training and Equipment Implications" (San Marcos, TX: Advanced Law Enforcement Rapid Response Training, Texas State University, 2010), *http://policeforum.org/library/critical-issues-in-policing-series/Blair-UnitedStatesActiveShooterEventsfrom2000to2010Report-Final.pdf* (accessed April 24, 2013).

[2] Ibid.

[3] White House, "Now is the Time; the President's plan to protect our children and our communities by reducing gun violence," *http://www.whitehouse.gov/issues/preventing-gun-violence* (accessed April 25, 2013).

[4] VALOR is a U.S. attorney general initiative that addresses the increase in assaults and violence against law enforcement. For additional information, see *http://www.valorforblue.org/Home.*

[5] John Nicoletti, "Detection and Disruption of Insider/Outsider Perpetrated Violence" (lecture, Colorado Emergency Preparedness Partnership, December 2012).

[6] Oak Creek Police Department, "After-Action Report, Sikh Temple Shooting, Oak Creek, Wisconsin, August 5, 2012"; Colleen Curry, Michael James, Richard Esposito, and Jack Date, "7 Dead at Sikh Temple in Oak Creek, Wisconsin: Officials Believe 'White Supremacist' Behind 'Domestic Terrorism,'" ABC News,*http://abcnews.go.com/US/sikh-temple-oak-creek-wisconsin-officials-white-supremacist/story?id=16933779#.UXk4xkqyDGo* (accessed April 25, 2013).

[7] Federal Bureau of Investigation, "Survival Skills," For additional information, see *http://www.fbi.gov/about-us/training/letts* (accessed April 25, 2013).

[8] New York City Police Department, "Active Shooter: Recommendations and Analysis for Risk Mitigation, "*http://www.nyc.gov/html/nypd/downloads/pdf/cou nterterrorism/ActiveShooter.pdf* (accessed April 24, 2013).
[9] Ibid.
[10] Ibid.
[11] John Nicoletti, "Detection and Disruption of Insider/Outsider Perpetrated Violence."
[12] New York City Police Department, "Active Shooter."
[13] Blair and Martaindale, "United States Active Shooter Events."
[14] Ibid.
[15] Ibid.
[16] Oak Creek Police Department; Lieutenant Paul Vance.
[17] Blair and Martaindale, "United States Active Shooter Events."
[18] Ibid.

DISCUSSION QUESTION

1. Do you think that law-enforcement agencies in your local community (campus or municipal) have obtained the FBI training for active shooters as described in this article?

CRITICAL THINKING EXERCISE

If you were developing a comprehensive "active-shooter" training program for a borough or campus law enforcement agency, what do you think the elements of the training program should include? Make sure to reference violence risk assessment, needs assessment, critical training components, and methods of maintaining perishable skills.

EXECUTIVE SUMMARY: CHANGING COURSE
PREVENTING GANG MEMBERSHIP

By Nancy M. Ritter, Thomas R. Simon, Ph.D.,
and Reshma R. Mahendra, M.P.H.

National Institute of Justice and
U.S. Department of Health and Human Services
(2013)

INTERVENTION AND SUPPRESSION EFFORTS BY LAW enforcement are not sufficient to solve the youth gang problem in the U.S. To realize a significant and lasting reduction in youth gang activity, those who make decisions about how limited resources are allocated — as well as practitioners like teachers and police officers, community service providers and health care workers — must understand what the evidence shows about *preventing* young people from joining a gang in the first place. The gang problem in the United States peaked in the late 1990s. Although it started to decline after that, the youth gang problem increased from 2001 to 2005 and has remained stubbornly persistent over the past decade. Here are the facts:

- One in three local law enforcement agencies in 2010 reported youth gang problems in their jurisdiction.[1]
- In a 2010 national survey, 45 percent of high school students and 35 percent of middle schoolers said that there were gangs — or students who considered themselves part of a gang — in their school.[2]

- Nearly one in 12 young people said they belonged to a gang at some point during their teenage years.3 The challenge is how we can reduce gang-joining during a time of substantially limited national, state and local budgets. To help meet this challenge, the Centers for Disease Control and Prevention (CDC) and the National Institute of Justice (NIJ) formed a partnership to publish a book, *Changing Course: Preventing Gang Membership*. This executive summary highlights the book's chapters, which were written by some of the nation's top criminal justice and public health researchers.

THE CONSEQUENCES OF GANG MEMBERSHIP

The consequences of gangs — and the burden they place on the law enforcement and health systems in our communities — are significant. Homicide is the second leading cause of death for American adolescents and young adults, accounting for an average of 13 deaths every day among 15- to 24-year-olds.4

However, the number of violent deaths tells only part of the story. More than 700,000 young people are treated in emergency departments in the U.S. for assault-related injuries every year.4 Although kids in gangs are far more likely than kids not involved in gangs to be both victims and perpetrators of violence,5,6 the risks go far beyond crime and violence. Gang-involved youth are more likely to engage in substance abuse and high-risk sexual behavior and to experience a wide range of potentially long-term health and social consequences, including school dropout, teen parenthood, family problems and unstable employment.7

WHY PREVENTION?

The large majority of youth who join a gang do so at a very early age: between 11 and 15 years old, with the peak years between 13 and 15.8 Therefore, early prevention is key. However, local, state and federal budgets in many arenas — including public health, criminal justice, education and community services — are currently addressing the *aftermath* of gang-joining on individual youth and their families, schools and communities. Fortunately, we know that many early prevention programs are effective *and* provide taxpayers with significantly more benefits than costs.

Nobel Prize-winning economist James Heckman, for example, has written about the economic benefits of targeting high-risk children before they start kindergarten.[9] Researchers at the Washington State Institute for Public Policy have done cost-benefit analyses of prevention programs that show significant effects on a range of outcomes, including crime, educational attainment, substance abuse, child abuse and neglect, teen pregnancy and public assistance.[10] Many programs have substantial returns that far exceed the costs. Hence, the focus of *Changing Course* is on the early prevention of gang-joining.

How Big Is the Problem?

In the first chapter of *Changing Course*, James C. ("Buddy") Howell discusses the magnitude of the gangs problem in the U.S. and why preventing kids from joining gangs is so important. "At the individual level," Dr. Howell writes, "youth who join a gang develop an increased propensity for violence and, in turn, are more likely to be victims of violence. In addition, the likelihood of favorable life-course outcomes is significantly reduced. Communities are also negatively affected by gangs, particularly in terms of quality of life, crime, victimization and the economic costs." Howell discusses how gang involvement encourages more active participation in delinquency, drug use, drug trafficking and violence — all of which, in turn, may result in arrest, conviction and incarceration.[11,12]

Gang involvement also tends to bring disorder to the life course in a cumulative pattern of negative outcomes, including school dropout, teen parenthood and unstable employment.[13] With respect to community decline and other costs, Howell reports that large cities have seen consistently high or increasing levels of gang-related homicides in recent years.[14] He also discusses other impacts on communities, including losses in property values, neighborhood businesses and tax revenue; weakened informal social control mechanisms; and an exodus of families from gang-ridden neighborhoods.[15]

The cost of crime to Americans has been estimated at $655 billion each year[16] and, over the course of his or her lifetime, a high-rate criminal offender can impose an estimated $4.2–7.2 million in costs on society.[17,18] Howell notes, however, that the costs are relatively low during the *early* years of the life of a chronic offender (defined as six or more police contacts by age 26) — about $3,000 by age 10.[17] This, he argues, highlights the cost benefits of early prevention efforts that focus on youth in high-risk settings before problem behaviors develop.

The evidence, says Howell, is that the most successful anti-gang initiatives are communitywide in scope, have broad community involvement in planning and delivery, and employ integrated outreach support and services. He concludes with words of hope: "[C]ommunities that organize and mobilize themselves using a data-driven strategy can direct their resources toward effectively preventing gang formation and its associated criminal activity."

THE ATTRACTIONS OF GANGS
Carl S. Taylor and Pamela R. Smith argue that policymakers and practitioners must understand that, to some kids, the positive aspects of being in a gang seem to outweigh the potentially life-destroying consequences. In their chapter in *Changing Course,* Dr. Taylor and Ms. Smith discuss:

ECONOMICS
Today's economic reality can often leave teenagers out of the labor market — and the promise of material reward is a significant attraction for kids who join gangs.[19-22] For many young people who feel disconnected from the American Dream, say Taylor and Smith, the economic opportunities of gang membership offer an acceptable alternative to a low-wage job in the legitimate employment arena.[19,23,24]

A SUPPORT SYSTEM AND SENSE OF BELONGING
Youth who feel marginalized, rejected or ignored in the family, school or church may join a gang to fill a need for support.[22] Some youth join a gang for a sense of belonging, viewing the gang as a substitute or auxiliary family.[20,22,25] "I was in the gang," said Yusuf Shakur, now the director of Detroit's Urban Youth Leadership Group, whom Taylor and Smith interviewed for *Changing Course.* "What lured me was ... there was guys who made me feel like I was something special. They were my

brothers; they looked out for me. If you want change, you have to compete with that fact."

RELATIONSHIPS WITH FAMILY AND FRIENDS

For some, the appeal is that a friend or family member is already in the gang.[6, 22] Youth who have older family members who are in a gang may feel particularly motivated to join.

PROTECTION

There is incontrovertible evidence that kids in a gang are more likely to be exposed to violence than kids who do not belong to a gang. However, that truth does not resonate with many kids who join a gang, believing that it protects them from violence in school or the community. Some youth also seek the protection of a gang because of problems at home.[20] Girls who experience physical or sexual abuse at home may believe that being in a gang offers them protection.[26]

STATUS

For at-risk adolescents, gangs can be seen as a way to increase their status among peers. For these youth, joining a gang can also be regarded as a way to get respect, freedom and independence — all self-empowerment factors that may be missing from their lives.

OUTLAW MENTALITY

Many kids — not only those at risk for gang membership — rebel against traditional societal values. For some, running with an organization of gangsters, hoodlums, thugs or banditos seems to be taking a stand against society. Taylor and Smith argue that it is important to understand the image of an "outlaw culture" during the cognitive development stage of adolescence.

THE NEXUS OF PUBLIC SAFETY AND PUBLIC HEALTH

Public health and public safety workers who respond to gang problems know that after-the-fact efforts are not enough. An emergency department doctor who treats gang-related gunshot wounds or a police officer who must tell a mother that her son has been killed in a drive-by shooting is likely to stress the need for prevention — and the complementary roles that public health and law enforcement must play — in stopping violence before it starts.

As a joint NIJ-CDC publication, *Changing Course* exemplifies the nexus of public safety and public health. In the book's conclusion, the two federal research agencies extend an invitation to policymakers and practitioners to engage in a new way of thinking about the intersection of public health and public safety and leveraging resources. Indeed, the need to think more broadly about gang-joining is one of the reasons CDC and NIJ brought together diverse perspectives — from public health and law enforcement, and from researchers and practitioners.

THE ROLE OF PUBLIC HEALTH

Gang membership has traditionally been viewed from a public safety — rather than a public health —perspective. In *Changing Course,* however, Tamara M. Haegerich and her co-authors, James Mercy and Billie Weiss, say that looking at the issue solely through the public safety lens fails to leverage the extensive expertise of our nation's public health professionals, who understand the impact on the health of an individual gang member *and* on the health of a community. Based on a cross-disciplinary principle that puts everybody — medical and mental health, criminal justice, education and social services — at the table, the public health approach uses four steps:

- Describe and monitor the problem.
- Identify the risk and protective factors.
- Develop and evaluate prevention strategies.
- Ensure widespread implementation.

Although the public health model is ideal for developing programs to help prevent kids from joining gangs, it does not come without challenges. One is that, in many respects, the idea of "prevention" is not understood or highly valued by our society. Community leaders are strongly invested in strategies that focus on holding perpetrators accountable and that supposedly yield immediate results, as described by Dr. Haegerich and her colleagues.

Preventing gang violence through reductions in gang membership will require a long-term investment in research, program development and evaluation, they write. Public health can contribute to the development of definitions, data elements and data systems that can help the nation understand the magnitude of gang-joining and violence. Indeed, the public health approach to monitoring trends, researching risk and protective factors, evaluating interventions, and supporting the dissemination and implementation of evidence-based strategies is an important complement to law enforcement.

However, as Haegerich and her co-authors write, communities often lack a comprehensive gang-joining prevention strategy that includes public health departments and public health professionals. "With some notable exceptions," they say, "state and local health departments have been reluctant to tackle the issue of violence prevention, much less gang violence prevention or gang-joining prevention." This may be due to a variety of factors, such as lack of funding support. As a result, the authors argue, "[T]he prevention system needed to support and sustain successful dissemination and implementation of programs and policies does not presently exist in most locales." Haegerich and her co-authors call for fundamental operational changes in agencies and systems — as well as coordination of funding streams — to facilitate collaboration across sectors and generate sufficient resources to monitor gang membership and to implement and evaluate prevention strategies.

THE ROLE OF LAW ENFORCEMENT

Scott Decker writes in *Changing Course* that to prevent kids from joining gangs, we must move beyond a "hook 'em and book 'em" mentality. Police, he says, must enhance their traditional role as crime fighters by collaborating — with public health, school, community, and other public- and private-sector partners — on primary, front-end prevention strategies.

Dr. Decker argues that the mandate for police to play a key role in gang prevention is clear. "The police have a vital role in *preventing* youth from joining gangs in the first place," he says. "In fact, they have a true mandate with respect to efforts to prevent gang-joining: It is, quite simply, a part of their job to serve and protect."

Decker describes how gangs disrupt the important socializing power of the very institutions that help young people learn and abide by the appropriate rules of a society: family, school and community. Not only do gang members commit crimes — victimizing innocents and each other — but their presence detracts from a neighborhood's quality of life. Gangs also divert important resources — money, personnel, programs and attention — from other activities that could help create healthier, more productive communities.

Although the police already engage in a considerable number of prevention activities, Decker says that their role in preventing kids from joining gangs could — and should — be enhanced through use of the Scanning, Analyzing, Responding, Assessing (SARA) model. SARA goes beyond the response to 911 calls for service by (1) scanning the environment for crime problems, (2) analyzing problems through multiple sources of information, (3) developing a response, and (4) assessing the effectiveness of the response.

Police can play a crucial role in a community's effort to prevent kids from joining gangs by gathering better knowledge of where gang problems exist and who is vulnerable to membership. Decker writes that, in this regard, patrolling is important — and, because officers are already doing this, it doesn't cost more money. Law enforcement leadership should emphasize, reinforce and reward the prevention aspects of patrolling, Decker says.

The chapter also discusses how crucial police partnerships with other community players are in any gang-prevention initiative. Finally, Decker notes that working in collaboration on efforts to prevent gang-joining increases police legitimacy and credibility, particularly in at-risk communities and among at-risk youth. "Police legitimacy can be increased through partnerships with community groups and agencies that are trying to reduce the attraction of gangs; when police play a more active, visible role in gang-membership prevention activities, it builds trust and improves community efficacy," he writes. The bottom line is that neighborhoods and communities with high collective efficacy have a greater ability to regulate the behavior of their juveniles, which, in turn, helps prevent gang-joining.

UNDERSTANDING THE ROLE OF CHILD DEVELOPMENT

The promise of prevention is that most youth — even those most at risk, living in the most distressed urban communities — do *not* join a gang. The question, therefore, is: Why do some? Every decision we make is influenced by contexts that develop over time, and joining a gang is no different, says Nancy G. Guerra. "A 13-year-old does not wake up one day and decide out of the blue to join a gang," Dr. Guerra and her colleagues, Carly B. Dierkhising and Pedro R. Payne, write in *Changing Course*. "The decision is a consequence of a particular life environment, behavior and way of thinking that leads a child to adopt the gang lifestyle later on." Their chapter delves into the individual and family factors in early childhood (ages 0–5) and during the elementary school years (ages 6–12) that increase the risk for gang-joining. "Gang intervention strategies often focus on adolescents," Guerra and her co-authors write, "but to help prevent youth from joining a gang, it is important that practitioners and policymakers address the developmental needs of youth from birth (or even prenatally) to age 12."

Joining a gang should be understood as part of a life course that begins when a child is born (or before). Important risk factors for children ages 0–5 include hypervigilance to threat, cognitive impairments, insecure attachment to a caregiver and early aggressive behavior.[27-31] For 6- to 12-year-olds, important risk factors include poor school performance and parental monitoring, deficits in social information-processing skills, antisocial beliefs, and negative relationships with peers, including being rejected and victimized by peers.[32-35]

Because the age of 12 (which roughly corresponds with the transition from elementary to middle school) can be a crucial *turning point* where lifestyle decisions are made, it is very important to begin prevention early in life, "before harmful lifestyle decisions are made and before transient behaviors in childhood, such as aggression, turn into habits that are hard to break," the authors argue. "We know," they write, "that children are at risk for joining a gang from an early age if they are hyper-sensitive to threat because they regularly see shootings in the neighborhood, have fallen behind in school because they can't read, or live in neighborhoods where gangs and 'easy money' seem to go hand-in-hand." There are protective factors, however, that can help youth who are growing up in high-risk communities; these include higher levels of social-emotional competence, academic success, secure attachment and effective parenting.

In *Changing Course,* Guerra and her colleagues explore ways to identify at-risk youth and provide them with age-appropriate prevention strategies, such as those that improve family functioning and connections with schools, facilitate involvement with socially appropriate peers, and reduce bullying and victimization. Such programs can help them avoid a cascade of problems, including gang-joining, delinquency and violence.

THE ROLE OF FAMILIES

Deborah Gorman-Smith and her colleagues, Andrea Kampfner and Kimberly Bromann, discuss how early prevention strategies can increase the protective role of families in preventing gang-joining. We know, for example, that aggressive and antisocial behavior during childhood is a risk factor for crime, violence and gang involvement later in life. In general, the earlier that youth join a gang, the greater the severity of involvement. The age of onset, in turn, tends to be related to family functioning. Serious disruptions in parenting and family functioning are related to earlier onset of delinquent behavior, which is generally more severe and dangerous than when criminal activity begins later in adolescence.[36]

Effective parenting and strong family functioning — with warm affective bonds, high monitoring and consistent discipline — protect against a variety of antisocial and problem behaviors, such as involvement with delinquent peers and subsequent likelihood of gang membership and violence. "Particularly for families living in high-risk neighborhoods, programs that help to build networks of social support and foster family-community ties can provide an additional protective factor to support healthy development and prevent youth involvement in gang and other types of violence," Dr. Gorman-Smith and her co-authors say.

Very early prevention is possible. For example, among the most promising evidence-based prevention programs are those focused on providing support and assistance to low-income pregnant mothers and to families with young children. Practitioners, policymakers and prevention scientists need to coordinate efforts for scaling up and disseminating evidence-based, family-focused programs, the authors write. Although the path toward gang involvement is complicated — with, as Gorman-Smith and her colleagues note, "multiple determinants and no easy answers for prevention" — strengthening the family can help protect a child who is at risk of joining a gang.

THE ROLE OF SCHOOLS

Gary D. Gottfredson describes the need to increase the ability — and the willingness — of schools to accurately assess gang problems, implement prevention strategies, and address the fear in schools that contributes to the risk for gang-joining. Indeed, Dr. Gottfredson argues, providing a safe environment to ensure that students are not fearful may be the single most important thing schools can do to prevent gang-joining. "Communities must prevent gang problems and provide safe school environments not only to protect students and improve their educational outcomes but also to forestall a cycle in which school disorder and community disorganization perpetuate each other," he writes.

Arguing that many principals in schools with gang problems do not recognize or admit a problem, Gottfredson points to a large study of secondary schools, which found that only one-fifth of the principals of schools with gang problems (defined as more than 15 percent of students reporting they belonged to a gang) said their school had a problem.[37]

Gottfredson underscores the need for educational leaders to implement programs that make efficient use of educational time, use state-of-the-art methods, and have been shown to be effective in preventing problem behavior or gang involvement. Leaders must also be certain the programs are implemented as designed. Gottfredson says that, despite their potential to reduce the risk for problem behavior and violence in the general population when implemented well, school-based programs are unlikely to reach youth who are at greatest risk of gang-joining because many have dropped out or are not fully engaged in school.

In places with staggering dropout rates such as Baltimore (41 percent), Albuquerque (49 percent) and Philadelphia (61 percent),38 it is unrealistic, he says, to expect that school-based programs will reach the youth who are most at risk. "Much of the dropout occurs in the ninth grade, which means that youths at risk of dropout — who are typically poor school attendees while they remain enrolled —have little chance of exposure to programs in high school," he writes.

Gottfredson also notes that although alternate strategies, such as evening programs, may be helpful in reaching a fraction of this population, rigorous research on the efficacy of such approaches is lacking. The chapter discusses the importance of grounding school-based gang-prevention programs on a careful consideration of specific needs. Assessments of gang risks as well as the usefulness of current prevention activities are necessary to guide future action.

Systematic self-report surveys regarding gang involvement and victimization should be used to supplement existing data collection — such as school- or principal-reported incident or suspension rates — which are insufficient to develop a true picture of gang problems in schools. Schools can use this information to make decisions about which risk factors for gang-joining — including substance abuse, delinquency and violence — are most prevalent, choose programs that are known to reduce those risks, and then fully implement those programs.

THE ROLE OF COMMUNITIES

Because of a heavy emphasis on school-based programs, communities have largely been overlooked as a valuable resource in reaching kids who are at risk of joining a gang. Too often, says Jorja Leap, programs in the classroom are not connected to what is going on in the streets. This disconnect can be exacerbated by a feeling in the community that a "solution" is being imposed on them from the outside, but this paradigm must change, Dr. Leap argues.

In her discussion on the role of communities in preventing gang-joining, Leap says that, in today's economic reality — where budget cuts have reduced or entirely eliminated youth development programs — community partnerships must be a priority. Emphasizing the need for comprehensive approaches that enhance "core activities" such as tutoring, mentoring, life-skills training, case management, parental involvement, connection with schools, supervised recreational activities and community mobilization, Leap outlines key strategies, including:

- Avoid reinventing the wheel by building on programs that already exist.
- Develop strategic plans.
- Identify real and imagined boundaries.
- Make community participation a priority and maximize partnerships.
- Use training and technical assistance to expand organizational capacity.
- Ensure sustainability. Emphasizing opportunities to build on a community's existing strengths, Leap describes the need for multifaceted prevention efforts
- that are grounded in collaboration among the various stakeholders. She discusses how communities can conduct a needs assessment, choose the right partners and eliminate bureaucratic obstacles. The hard reality is that many community-based gang-prevention programs depend on a single or a small number of funding sources, Leap concludes. Because sustaining effective programs requires a continuing funding stream, building partnerships can be crucial.

PREVENTING GIRLS FROM JOINING GANGS

Until recently, girls in gangs were often "invisible," says Meda Chesney-Lind. One reason for this is that girls enter gangs — and exit from gang activity — at earlier ages than boys. In *Changing Course,* Dr. Chesney-Lind discusses families that are unable to support female adolescent development and provide basic safety. This — in conjunction with dangerous neighborhoods, possible sexual and other abuse, and poor-quality schools — paints a daunting picture for girls who are at risk of joining a gang. Girls in gangs are far more likely than their non-gang peers to have been sexually assaulted, generally by a family member.[39, 40]

In one study, researchers found that 62 percent of female gang members had been sexually abused or assaulted, and three-fourths said they had been physically abused.[41] Although girls join gangs for many of the same reasons as boys, girls are more likely to be seeking safety and security that they cannot find in a troubled or abusive home. Some girls join gangs in search of a surrogate family; others turn to a gang as a solution to family violence, believing that the gang may equip them to fight back physically or emotionally.[42] The reality, however, is that a gang is not a good place for protection.

Not only do girls experience higher levels of delinquency once in a gang but they can be raped during initiation.[43,44] Being in a gang significantly increases delinquent behavior for girls, as it does for boys. Chesney-Lind argues that early gang-joining prevention should focus on children who are at the greatest risk of neglect or abuse.

There should also be a focus on helping girls stay in school and avoid substance abuse and abusive boyfriends, and on giving them the skills to delay early sexual activity and parenthood. "Such work will be challenging, however, given years of inattention to girls' programming and the consequent lack of robust, gender-informed program models," she says. "We urgently need strategies to help the girls who are at the greatest risk for gang-joining, particularly those who may turn to a gang for 'protection' or a sense of belonging."

THE ROLE OF RACE AND ETHNICITY IN GANG-JOINING

Adrienne Freng and Terrance J. Taylor look at the complex role that race and ethnicity can play in gang membership, concluding that, although more research is needed, common underlying risk factors — such as poverty, challenges for immigrants, discrimination and social isolation — should be the focus at this point. "The roles of race and ethnicity in gang membership are becoming increasingly complicated, and it is important to understand that the term *gang membership* is not 'code' for race or ethnicity," they write in *Changing Course*. "The truth is that more and more gangs include white gang members and are becoming multiracial."

Drs. Freng and Taylor argue that there has long existed a connection between race/ethnicity and gang membership. Early gang members traditionally came from white ethnic immigrant groups, such as the Irish and Polish. Starting in the 1950s, however, gang membership has been increasingly concentrated among racial and ethnic minorities such as African-Americans, Hispanics and, increasingly, Asian and American Indian groups[45–50] — although there are a considerable number of white gang members as well.[51–53]

Emerging gangs have also become much more multiracial, which affects the role that race and ethnicity play in gang-joining, especially with respect to conflicts between gangs.[54] But do we need race-or ethnic-*specific* programming to help prevent gang-joining? Do we need more targeted programs that focus on specific risk factors for different racial and ethnic groups? Or is general gang-prevention programming — which includes some race- and ethnic-*sensitive* elements — sufficient?

Freng and Taylor point out that there is surprisingly little research to answer these questions. Noting some recent evidence that racial/ethnic-specific gang-prevention programming may not be necessary, the authors suggest that general prevention programming — which includes race- and ethnic-sensitive elements — may be helpful.[55] "To know whether race- and ethnic-*specific* programming would be more successful than general gang-prevention programming, it is important that current prevention programs be better evaluated to determine whether race or ethnicity has an impact on prevention efforts and outcomes," they say.

Freng and Taylor also argue that gang-prevention strategies should focus on "common denominators" that cut across racial and ethnic lines, such as poverty and immigration, social isolation and discrimination, drug use, limited educational opportunities and low parental monitoring. "We can act now on what we know about shared risk factors — poverty, immigration, discrimination, and social isolation — and their consequences in terms of substance abuse, limited educational and job opportunities, family stress, neighborhood crime and the influence of gangs — by implementing prevention programs that are racially, ethnically and culturally sensitive and are known to reduce relevant risks," they write.

EVALUATION: PREPARE TO PROVE SUCCESS

In a chapter on the importance of evaluation, Finn-Aage Esbensen and Kristy N. Matsuda say that, although it is no surprise that policymakers, practitioners and researchers have different mindsets when it comes to solving a problem, it is crucial that their thinking converges when it comes to determining whether a solution does (or does not) work. Everyone — from federal and state policymakers to local school board members, and from health departments to police departments — needs to be able to answer the question: "How do we *know* if we are preventing gang membership?" Anecdotal success stories do not justify creating a new program or continuing the investment in an ongoing one. Decisions should be made on the best available evidence. Therefore, it is crucial that decision-makers understand the key principles of process, outcome and cost-effectiveness evaluations.

A formal evaluation — of a strategy, initiative or program that is designed to prevent gang-joining — is the only way to measure outcomes and to understand what works and why it works. Drs. Esbensen and Matsuda say that, although many policymakers and practitioners understand that evaluation is critical to proving the success (or failure) of a program, most do not fully understand the role that evaluation plays in actually *designing* and *implementing* a successful gang-prevention program. "It is important that policymakers and practitioners understand the components of the most rigorous evaluations and, most important, be able to articulate to their constituents the real-world occurrences that sometimes make an outcome evaluation difficult to execute," they write. Esbensen and Matsuda describe the two basic types of evaluation: outcome and process. They also discuss the two strategies — cost-benefit analysis and cost-effectiveness analysis — for comparing the cost of a gang-prevention program with the cost of a criminal offender to society.

AN INVITATION

Changing Course extends an invitation to policymakers and practitioners to engage in a new way of thinking about the intersection of public health and public safety strategies and leveraging public health and public safety resources. Offering broad, strategic actions that can help reduce gang-joining and the violence and crime that often result, the conclusion of the book discusses six themes that span the individual chapters: (1) building partnerships, (2) using data, (3) framing the issue, (4) creating a plan, (5) implementing the plan, and (6) evaluating its effectiveness. The impacts of gang membership — and the burdens it places on our health, law enforcement, corrections, social and education systems — are significant.

However, there is reason for optimism. By preventing youth from joining gangs in the first place, we significantly improve their chances for a safe and productive life. That is why CDC and NIJ call the book *Changing Course: Preventing Gang Membership.* Faced with the current economic realities, prevention is the best way to halt the cascading impact of gangs on our kids, families, neighborhoods and society at large. By working together to focus on the prevention of gang membership, rather than solely caring for the victims of gang violence and arresting gang-involved youth, we can change the course of the future for our kids.

ABOUT THE AUTHORS

Nancy M. Ritter is a writer and editor at NIJ. Thomas R. Simon, Ph.D., is Deputy Associate Director for Science at CDC's Division of Violence Prevention. Reshma R. Mahendra, M.P.H., is a public health advisor at CDC's Division of Violence Prevention.

ENDNOTES

1. Egley A Jr, Howell JC. *Highlights of the 2010 National Youth Gang Survey.* Washington, DC: U.S. Department of Justice, Office of Justice Programs, Office of Juvenile Justice and Delinquency Prevention, 2012.
2. National Center on Addiction and Substance Abuse at Columbia University. *National Survey of American Attitudes on Substance Abuse XV: Teens and Parents, 2010.* New York, NY: National Center on Addiction and Substance Abuse at Columbia University, 2010.
3. Snyder HN, Sickmund M. *Juvenile Offenders and Victims: 2006 National Report.* Washington, DC: U.S. Department of Justice, Office of Justice

Programs, Office of Juvenile Justice and Delinquency Prevention, 2006. Available at www.ojjdp.gov/ojstatbb/nr2006.

4. Centers for Disease Control and Prevention. Web-based Injury Statistics Query and Reporting System (WISQARS) [online]. Centers for Disease Control and Prevention, National Center for Injury Prevention and Control, 2009. Available at www.cdc.gov/injury/wisqars/index.html. Accessed on Sept. 6, 2012.

5. Thornberry TP, Krohn MD, Lizotte AJ, Smith CA, Tobin K. *Gangs and Delinquency in Developmental Perspective.* New York, NY: Cambridge University Press, 2003.

6. Peterson D, Taylor TJ, Esbensen F-A. Gang membership and violent victimization. *Justice Quarterly* 2004; 21:793-815.

7. Krohn MD, Ward JT, Thornberry TP, Lizotte AJ, Chu R. The cascading effects of adolescent gang involvement across the life course. *Criminology* 2011; 49:991-1028.

8. Howell JC. *Gang Prevention: An Overview of Research and Programs.* Washington, DC: U.S. Department of Justice, Office of Justice Programs, Office of Juvenile Justice and Delinquency Prevention, 2010.

9. Heckman J. Skill formation and the economics in investing in disadvantaged children. *Science* 2006; 312:1900-1902.

10. See Washington State Institute for Public Policy's cost-benefit analyses at www.wsipp.wa.gov/ topic.asp?cat=18.

11. Krohn MD, Thornberry TP. Longitudinal perspectives on adolescent street gangs. In: Liberman A, ed., *The Long View of Crime: A Synthesis of Longitudinal Research.* New York, NY: Springer, 2008:128-160.

12. Howell MQ, Lassiter W. *Prevalence of Gang-Involved Youth in NC.* Raleigh, NC: North Carolina Department of Juvenile Justice and Delinquency Prevention, 2011.

13. Howell, JC. *Gangs in America's Communities.* Thousand Oaks, CA: Sage Publications, 2012.

14. Howell JC, Egley A Jr, Tita G, Griffiths E. U.S. gang problem trends and seriousness. *National Gang Center Bulletin.* No. 6. Tallahassee, FL: Institute for Intergovernmental Research, National Gang Center, 2011.

15. Decker SH, Pyrooz DC. Gang violence worldwide: Context, culture, and country. *Small Arms Survey 2010.* Geneva, Switzerland: Small Arms Survey, 2010.

16. Fight Crime: Invest in Kids. *Caught in the Crossfire: Arresting Gang Violence by Investing in Kids.* Washington, DC: Fight Crime: Invest in Kids, 2004.

17. Cohen MA, Piquero AR. New evidence on the monetary value of saving a high risk youth. *J Quant Criminol.* 2009; 25:25-49.

18. Cohen MA, Piquero AR, Jennings WG. Estimating the costs of bad outcomes for at-risk youth and the benefits of early childhood interventions to reduce them. *Crim Just Policy Rev.* 2010; 21:391-434.

19. Padilla F. *The Gang as an American Enterprise.* New Brunswick, NJ: Rutgers University Press, 1992.

20. Shelden RG, Tracy SK, Brown W. *Youth Gangs in American Society.* Belmont, CA: Wadsworth, 2004.

21. Taylor CS. *Dangerous Society.* East Lansing, MI: Michigan State University Press, 1990.

22. Wiener V. *Winning the War Against Youth Gangs: A Guide for Teens, Families, and Communities.* Westport, CT: Greenwood Press, 1999.

23. Brown WB. The fight for survival: African-American gang members and their families in a segregated society. *Juv Fam Court J.* 1998; 49:1-14.

24. Cureton SR. Introducing Hoover: I'll ride for you gangsta'. In: Huff CR, ed., *Gangs in America III.* Thousand Oaks, CA: Sage Publications, 2002:83-100.

25. Howell CJ. *Youth Gangs: An Overview.* Bulletin. Washington, DC: U.S. Department of Justice, Office of Justice Programs, Office of Juvenile Justice and Delinquency Prevention, 1998.

26. Miller J. The girls in the gang: What we've learned from two decades of research. In: Huff CR, ed., *Gangs in America III.* Thousand Oaks, CA: Sage Publications, 2002:183.

27. Cicchetti D, Rogosch FA, Gunnar MR, Toth SL. The differential impacts of early physical and sexual abuse and internalizing problems on daytime cortisol rhythm in school-aged children. *Child Dev.* 2010; 81:252-269.

28. Decker SH. Collective and normative features of gang violence. *Justice Q.* 1996; 13:243-264.

29. Fearon RP, Bakermans-Kranenburg MJ, Van Ijzendoorn MH, Lapsley AM, Roisman GI. The significance of insecure attachment and disorganization in the development of children's externalizing behavior: A meta-analytic study. *Child Dev.* 2010; 81:435-456.

30. Bowlby J. *Attachment and Loss, Vol. 2: Separation.* New York, NY: Basic Books, 1973.

31. Hill KG, Lui C, Hawkins JD. *Early Precursors of Gang Membership: A Study of Seattle Youth.* Washington, DC: U.S. Department of Justice, Office of Justice Programs, Office of Juvenile Justice and Delinquency Prevention, 2001.

32. Hill KG, Howell JC, Hawkins JD, Battin-Pearson SR. Childhood risk factors for adolescent gang membership: Results from the Seattle Social Development Project. *J Res Crime Delinq.* 1999; 36:300-322.

33. Huesmann LR, Guerra NG. Normative beliefs and the development of aggressive behavior. *J Pers Soc Psychol.* 1997; 72:1-12.

34. Fraser MW. Aggressive behavior in childhood and early adolescence: An ecological-developmental perspective on youth violence. *Soc Work* 1996; 41:347-361.

35. Robertson AA, Baird-Thomas C, Stein JA. Child victimization and parental monitoring as mediators of youth problem behaviors. *Crim Justice Behav.* 2008; 35:755-771.

36. Steinberg L. Familial factors in delinquency: A developmental perspective. *J Adolesc Res.* 1987; 2:255-268.

37. Gottfredson GD, Gottfredson DC. *Gang Problems and Gang Programs in a National Sample of Schools.* Ellicott City, MD: Gottfredson Associates, 2001.

38. Swanson CB. *Cities in Crisis 2009: Closing the Graduation Gap.* Bethesda, MD: Editorial Projects in Education, Inc., 2009.

39. Miller J. Young women in street gangs: Risk factors, delinquency, and victimization risk. In: Reed W, Decker SH, eds., *Responding to Gangs:*

Evaluation and Research. Washington, DC: U.S. Department of Justice, Office of Justice Programs, National Institute of Justice, 2002:68-105.

40. Esbensen F-A, Huizinga D. Gangs, drugs, and delinquency in a survey of youth. *Criminology* 1993; 31:565-589.

41. Joe K, Chesney-Lind M. Just every mother's angel: An analysis of gender and ethnic variations in youth gang membership. *Gend Soc.* 1995; 9(4):408-430.

42. Joe-Laidler K, Hunt G. Violence and social organization in female gangs. *Soc Justice* 1997; 24(4):148-169.

43. Cepeda A, Valdez A. Risk behaviors among young Mexican-American gang-associated females: Sexual relations, partying, substance use, and crime. *J Adolesc Res.* 2003; 18:90-106.

44. Portillos EL. The social construction of gender in the barrio. In: Chesney-Lind M, Hagedorn J, eds., *Female Gangs in America: Essays on Girls, Gangs and Gender.* Chicago, IL: Lake View Press, 1999:232-244.

45. Chin K-L. Gang violence in Chinatown. In: Huff CR, ed., *Gangs in America.* 2nd ed. Thousand Oaks, CA: Sage Publications, 1996:157-181.

46. Hagedorn JM. *People and Folks: Gangs, Crime, and the Underclass in a Rustbelt City.* Chicago, IL: Lake View Press, 1988.

47. Major AK, Egley Jr A, Howell JC, Mendenhall B, Armstrong T. *Youth Gangs in Indian Country.* Washington, DC: U.S. Department of Justice, Office of Justice Programs, Office of Juvenile Justice and Delinquency Prevention, 2004.

48. Moore J. *Going Down to the Barrio: Homeboys and Homegirls in Change.* Philadelphia, PA: Temple University Press, 1991.

49. Vigil JD. *Barrio Gangs: Street Life and Identity in Southern California.* Austin, TX: University of Texas Press, 1988.

50. Vigil JD. *A Rainbow of Gangs: Street Cultures in the Mega-City.* Austin, TX: University of Texas Press, 2002.

51. Esbensen F-A, Osgood DW. Gang Resistance Education and Training (G.R.E.A.T.): Results from the national evaluation. *J Res Crime Delinq.* 1999; 36:194-225.

52. Freng AL, Winfree Jr LT. Exploring race and ethnic differences in a sample of middle school gang members. In: Esbensen F-A, Tibbetts SG, Gaines L, eds., *American Youth Gangs at the Millennium.* Long Grove, IL: Waveland Press, 2004:142-162.

53. National Gang Center. *National Youth Gang Survey Analysis,* 2009 [online]. Available at www. nationalgangcenter.gov/Survey-Analysis. Accessed on January 25, 2010.

54. Starbuck D, Howell JC, Lindquist DJ. *Hybrid and Other Modern Gangs.* Washington, DC: U.S. Department of Justice, Office of Justice Programs, Office of Juvenile Justice and Delinquency Prevention, 2001.

55. Esbensen F-A, Peterson D, Taylor TJ, Freng A. *Youth Violence: Understanding the Role of Sex, Race/Ethnicity, and Gang Membership.* Philadelphia, PA: Temple University Press, 2010.

DISCUSSION QUESTION

1. From your perspective, what positive realistic efforts might actually make gang membership less attractive?

CRITICAL THINKING EXERCISE

As a group, indentify which criminological theories provide a good basis for understanding why young adults and teenagers join gangs. Next, discuss how an awareness of any factors or elements of these criminological theories—in conjunction with observations and/or recommendations found in this article—might contribute to *preventing* gang membership.

OTHER BOOKS BY DR. CENCICH

THE DEVIL'S GARDEN: A WAR CRIMES INVESTIGATOR'S STORY
POTOMAC BOOKS

ADVANCED CRIMINAL LAW AND INVESTIGATION
THE HAGUE PRESS INTERNATIONAL

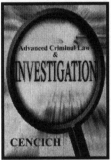

OFFENDER MOTIVATION AND VALUES:
HIGH SPEED ISSUES IN INTERNATIONAL SECURITY
THE HAGUE PRESS INTERNATIONAL

Made in the USA
Charleston, SC
23 December 2015